25 WA

THE
YORKSHIRE
DALES

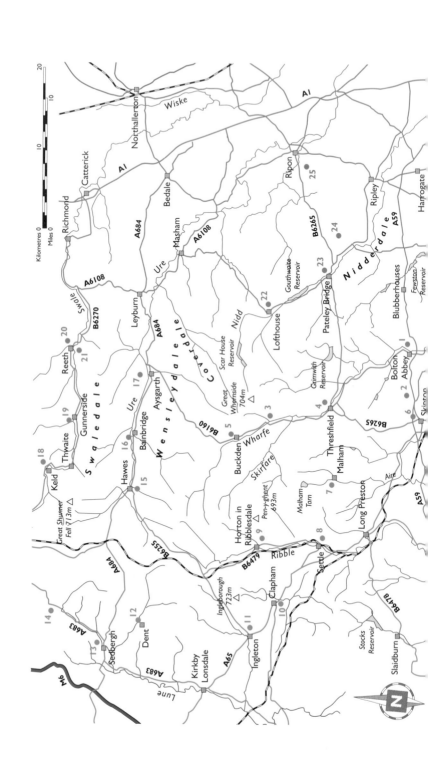

25 WALKS

THE
YORKSHIRE
DALES

Paul Hannon

Series Editor: Roger Smith

EDINBURGH:HMSO

First published 1996

Applications for reproduction should be made to HMSO

HMSO acknowledge with thanks access to and use of photographs
from—*Paul Hannon/Big Country Picture Library*.

British Library Cataloguing in Publication Data

A catalogue record for this book is available from the British Library

ISBN 0 11 495725 8

CONTENTS

USEFUL INFORMATION

The length of each walk is given in kilometres and miles, but within the text measurements are metric for simplicity. The walks are described in detail and are supported by accompanying maps (study them before you start the walk), so there is little likelihood of getting lost, but if you want a back-up you will find the 1:25 000 Outdoor Leisure and Pathfinder Ordnance Survey maps on sale locally.

Every care has been taken to make the descriptions and maps as accurate as possible, but the author and publishers can accept no responsibility for errors, however caused. The countryside is always changing and there will inevitably be alterations to some aspects of these walks as time goes by. The publishers and author would be happy to receive comments and suggested alterations for future editions of the book.

Yorkshire Dales National Park Information Services
Colvend, Hebden Road, Grassington, Skipton,
N. Yorkshire BD23 5LB
Tel. 01756 752748

National Park Centres
Note: Most centres are open Easter to the end of October, daily 1000–1600, and some winter weekends. Check locally for variations.
Grassington Tel: 01756 752774
Malham Tel: 01729 830363
Clapham Tel: 01524 251419
Sedbergh Tel: 01539 620125
Hawes Tel: 01969 667450
Aysgarth Falls Tel: 01969 663424

Bolton Abbey estate office Tel: 01756 710227

Yorkshire & Humberside Tourist Board
312 Tadcaster Road, York YO2 2HF, Tel: 01904 707961
Good range of literature giving general information and also accommodation guides.

METRIC MEASUREMENTS

At the beginning of each walk, the distance is given in miles and kilometres. Within the text, all measurements are metric for simplicity (and indeed our Ordnance Survey maps are now all metric). However, it was felt that a conversion table might be useful to those readers who, like the author, still tend to think in Imperial terms.

The basic statistic to remember is that one kilometre is five-eighths of a mile. Half a mile is equivalent to 800 metres and a quarter-mile is 400 metres. Below that distance, yards and metres are little different in practical terms.

km	miles
1	0.625
1.6	1
2	1.25
3	1.875
3.2	2
4	2.5
4.8	3
5	3.125
6	3.75
6.4	4
7	4.375
8	5
9	5.625
10	6.25
16	10

Tourist Information Centres
Note: opening may be seasonal. Most TICs are open from Easter to the end of
October. Check locally for variations.
9 Sheep Street, Skipton Tel. 01756 792809
Town Hall, Settle Tel. 01729 825192
Community Centre, Ingleton Tel. 01524 241049
Queens Road, Richmond Tel. 01748 850252
Penyghent Cafe, Horton in Ribblesdale Tel. 01729 860333
Thornborough Hall, Leyburn Tel. 01969 23069
Minster Road, Ripon Tel. 01765 604625
High Street, Pateley Bridge Tel. 01423 711147
Royal Baths Assembly Rooms, Harrogate Tel. 01423 525666

Yorkshire Dales Society
YDS is an amenity body campaigning for the conservation and sustainable use of
the Dales landscape and for the future of its communities. Publishes a regular
Newsletter and holds members events.
For enquiries contact the Society at Otley Civic Centre, Cross Green, Otley,
W Yorkshire LS21 1HD
Tel. 01943 607868

The National Trust
Regional Office:
Goddards, 27 Tadcaster Road, York YO2 2QG
Tel. 01904 702021

Dales Connections (comprehensive public transport timetables)
Elmtree Press & Distribution, The Elms, Exelby, Bedale,
North Yorkshire DL8 2HD (send 50p to cover post and packing).

INTRODUCTION

The Yorkshire Dales is the third largest of the National Parks in England and Wales, and is in every sense the true heart of the Pennine Chain. It encompasses the bulk of the central Pennines between the Aire Gap in the south and the Stainmore Gap in the north. In addition to the designated area, great expanses of National Park quality landscape adjoin, most notably to the east. Here the Nidderdale Moors have belatedly received recognition as an Area of Outstanding Natural Beauty. West of the Three Peaks and north of Sedbergh there are areas without even this protection: the odd situation of stepping out of a National Park into such an area occurs at many points. There is of course no visible evidence of a changed landscape quality, just a line on a map where an old county boundary once ran! The bottom line is this: there is more to the Yorkshire Dales than the National Park.

There can be few better regions for walking. The very diversity ensures there is rambling suitable for all ages and all levels of experience. The Dales are accessible too, with a railway line through the heart and others around the fringe. This fringe features a necklace of towns proclaiming themselves as gateways to the Dales. Skipton lays greatest claim, but the likes of Harrogate, Richmond and Kirkby Stephen also play a role.

So what of the walking opportunities? The limestone region in the south and west of the park is internationally renowned for its caves, waterfalls and gleaming white pavements and scars. Not only is the most dramatic scenery to be found here, but the shapeliest and best known fells also rise high above the limestone platforms. The Ingleton-Settle-Malham corner will undoubtedly leave a lasting impression.

Limestone country also extends eastwards into Wharfedale. By the time you get here, you'll be keenly aware of what a major part the villages play in the Dales scene. Linton, Arncliffe and Kettlewell, amongst others, are integral to the wonderful landscape. Above the monastic splendour of Bolton Abbey rise heather-carpeted moorlands, which are repeated on a far more extensive scale in Swaledale to the north.

The absorbing remains of the once all-embracing lead mining industry are also at their most evocative in Swaledale, with abandoned smelting mills lurking in deep gills. Again, particularly in Swaledale, the villages return to haunt you with their loveliness: the ghosts of lead miners who occupied what are now picture-postcard cottages at Muker and Gunnerside might also do their own haunting. Swaledale is perhaps best known, however, for its flower-rich meadows, which present a dazzling scene in early summer. While every dale boasts its own waterfalls, you won't find anything to match Wensleydale's remarkable collection. The dramatic corners of this big, green valley must be sought out, but they are most certainly there to be found.

The higher fells are broad tracts of lonely country scattered throughout the park, some with rugged gritstone caps and offering endless miles of rough grass walking.

The easiest fellwalking is found on the Howgill Fells, a delectable western corner of the district overlooking the little town of Sedbergh. Underlying slate brings a complete change of character to this compact group, resulting in user-friendly short-cropped turf covering countless high level ridges.

Not surprisingly, the walks are as varied as the landscape, and within these pages riverside paths interlink with more demanding ascents of the fells. Your steps will trace a wealth of ancient routeways, from packhorse trails and Roman roads to old tracks serving long defunct mines, quarries and peat and coal pits. Modern routes also feature, including sections of the Pennine Way, Coast to Coast Walk and Dales Way, the latter being the area's very own long distance trail. Though none begin or finish in the park, they all traverse it from end to end.

Virtually all rights of way within the National Park are signposted where they leave roads, and the waymarking along the paths is generally of a high standard. A yellow (footpath) or blue (bridleway) waymark or blob of paint will often be found to confirm the line of a route. In most cases the presence of well maintained wall-stiles gives further help. The paths outside the park, principally Nidderdale, are perhaps less well tended, but should not present any problems.

If an Ordnance Survey map is carried, then the 1:25,000 Outdoor Leisure series are the finest: the three Yorkshire Dales sheets cover the majority of the walks. For general planning purposes, the 1 inch to 1 mile (1:63,000) sheet 'Yorkshire Dales Touring Map and Guide' is ideal. It covers all but two of the walks. I hope you enjoy these walks as much as I have while putting this guide together.

PAUL HANNON

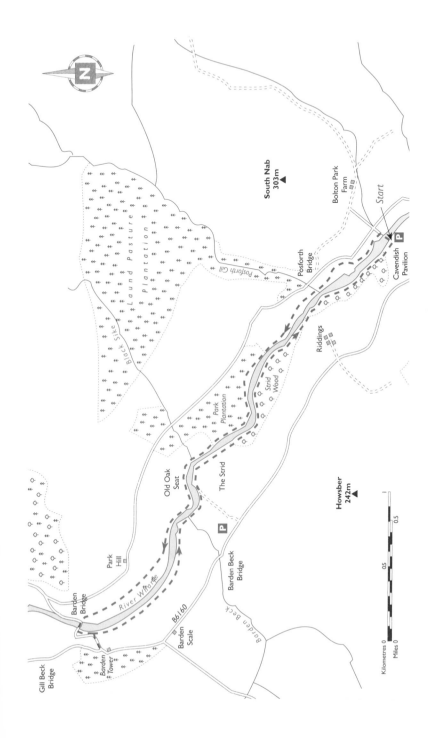

A STRID WOOD STRIDE

The walk features an outstanding juxtaposition of river and woodland, and an absolute riot of autumn colour.

This delectable section of the Wharfe is part of the Duke of Devonshire's Bolton Abbey estate, and a combination of public footpaths and permissive paths allows good access to both banks. Paths along the west bank have been incorporated into nature trails, and a locally available leaflet helps to unravel the colour codes.

Other than at the Strid, however, it is the woodland itself that steals the show from the river. Strid Wood is a hugely popular riverside habitat where man and nature co-exist with little difficulty. The importance of the woodland for bird and plant life has been recognised by designation as a Site of Scientific Interest (SSSI) and this should be respected by keeping to the paths. The splendid network laid out during the 19th century has been well maintained ever since.

From the Pavilion, cross the wooden bridge and turn upstream: shortly after entering woods the path is forced up near a road to negotiate Posforth Gill, but immediately returns to the wooded bank. It clings to the river until presented with a fork, where a simple choice is complicated by the respective attractions of either branch. The lower path is at times an exciting clamber over water-washed rocks, and caution is needed if the river is high: the path runs past the Strid to eventually meet the higher path.

Firmly recommended is the higher level option, despite its surprisingly sustained pull to the

INFORMATION

Distance: 10 km (6 miles).

Start and finish: Cavendish Pavilion, Bolton Abbey. Situated just north of the village on the B6160. There is a large car park signposted off the road: fee payable.

Terrain: Riverside walking, good paths but can be wet and rough underfoot. Boots advisable.

Public transport: Bolton Abbey is served by bus from Skipton.

Refreshments: Cafe at the start; often an ice cream van midway, in summer.

Opening hours: *Bolton Priory:* all reasonable hours, free.

Wharfe, Barden.

top of the wood. Hereafter, easy walking ensues along a magnificent terrace. Although a couple of paths later break off down to the river, the only point of any possible doubt occurs just after the climb, keeping left at a crossroads to pass a rest-house. Bedecked with a luxuriant bilberry thatch, the up-market rest-house is sited at the first of many well chosen viewpoints on the high path. One particular glimpse gives a surprise cameo of the Strid, perfectly framed by foliage. Shortly afterwards comes another classic, as the High Strid is revealed in a contrastingly open setting. On re-uniting, the path leaves the wood to run past a sturdy aqueduct to arrive at Barden Bridge.

Those with time to spare will enjoy a detour up the road after crossing the bridge, for just two minutes above are the ruins of Barden Tower. It was built as a hunting lodge by the Cliffords of Skipton Castle, and boasted two famous residents from that family. Henry the 'Shepherd' Lord came in 1485, being raised in the Cumbrian fells until the end of the Wars of the Roses. Up to his death in 1523 he preferred Barden's peace and the company of the canons of Bolton to the

Barden Tower.

splendour of Skipton. He also had the adjacent chapel built. The indomitable Lady Anne had the tower restored in 1659 and spent much of her final years here, a stone tablet on an exterior wall surviving to confirm her work. In 1676 she died, last of the Cliffords, and the long process of decay began.

Back at the bridge a stile kicks off the return leg, soon emerging from trees for another grassy spell past the aqueduct. On entering Strid Wood a network of nature trail paths give a colourful choice, though the main path is obvious throughout. An early detour stays nearest the river to savour the High Strid and a rock pinnacle – the Hawkstone – above the rocky path. Either way the Strid itself, further downstream, cannot be missed. Here is

The Strid.

the focal point of the wood, as the Wharfe is forced through a narrow gritstone channel of great depth. Lives have been lost here in senseless attempts to leap the foaming waters. Many decades ago visitors could travel here in style, by wagonette from the old railway station, along the broad carriageway that leads you gently back to the Cavendish Pavilion.

Paths downstream on either bank lead to the priory itself, open at all times: a footbridge allows a circular extension to be enjoyed. Bolton Abbey is, strictly, the name for the tiny village whose showpiece is more correctly the Priory. The imposing ruins occupy a glorious setting on the Wharfe's green bank – an attraction in its own right – and together form a magnet for close-at-hand West Yorkshire visitors. The priory dates from 1154 and was built by Augustinian canons who moved here from nearby Embsay. At the Dissolution, the nave was spared, and remains to this day the parish church. Further interest is provided by the adjacent Bolton Hall dating from the 17th century; while by the Post Office is a large and splendid example of a tithe barn.

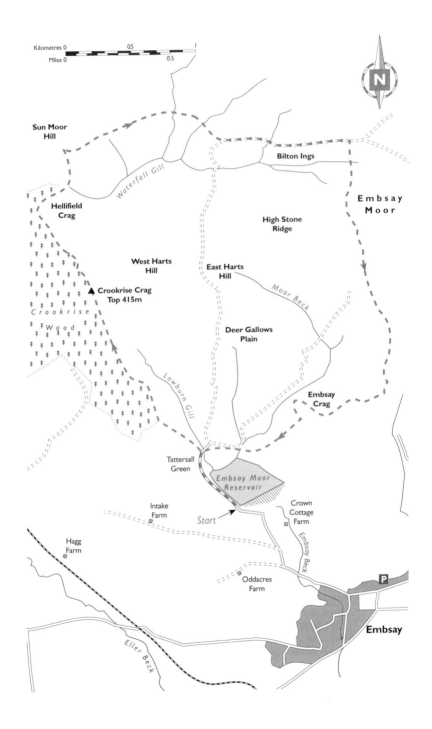

Kilometres 0   0.5   1
Miles 0   0.5

N

Sun Moor
Hill

Waterfall Gill

Bilton Ings

Embsay
Moor

Hellifield
Crag

High Stone
Ridge

West Harts
Hill

East Harts
Hill

Moor Beck

▲ Crookrise Crag
Top 415m

Crookrise

Wood

Deer Gallows
Plain

Lowburn Gill

Embsay
Crag

Tattersall
Green

Embsay Moor
Reservoir

Intake
Farm

Start

Crown
Cottage
Farm

Hagg
Farm

Embsay Beck

P

Oddacres
Farm

Embsay

Eller Beck

THE HEATHER HEIGHTS OF BARDEN MOOR

Embsay Moor is part of the splendid mass of heather upland that is all-embracing Barden Moor. Part of the Duke of Devonshire's estates, it has been a willing party to an access agreement for several decades, and is the perfect evidence in the case for walkers and grouse co-existing. Embsay Moor Reservoir has a fine setting under Embsay Crag and the moor itself.

Under Embsay Crag.

From the car park, head along the stony track outside the reservoir wall, past the sailing club to the far end. Here a stile leads onto the open moor. Turn left onto a path beginning an immediate climb, soon accompanying a wall. Remaining near the wall, the path further improves and passes through characterful bouldery scenery before levelling out. Soon a stile in the wall is reached: use it to attain the top of the cliffs of Crookrise, a breathtaking moment.

The panorama stretches across Craven from the Aire Valley to the South Pennine moors and Pendle Hill. Beyond are the Bowland moors, and then the Malhamdale hills intervene. Flasby Fell's tops are directly in front, while the higher reaches of the Dales fill the scene to the north. Confined between the steep drop and the wall, continue northwards to the Ordnance Survey column which soon appears. At

INFORMATION

Distance: 9 km (6 miles).

Start and finish: Embsay. Start from the Water Authority car park at Embsay Moor Reservoir (Grid ref. SD 998544), reached by Pasture Road off Elm Tree Square at the top of the village.

Terrain: Paths and tracks on heathery moorland. Some boggy sections, boots recommended.

Public transport: Embsay is served by bus from Skipton.

Refreshments: Pubs in Embsay, nothing en route.

Please note: Much of this route is not on public rights of way, but on a negotiated access area. As such, it is liable to closure at times of high fire risk, and on a limited number of days (not Sundays) during the grouse shooting season (starting August 12th). If in doubt contact the estate or a National Park Centre. Closure notices are also posted at all access points. Please also note that dogs are not permitted off the rights of way on the access area.

415m, this is Crookrise Crag Top. Barden Moor comes to an abrupt halt at many places around its rim, but nowhere as dramatic as Crookrise, where a line of crags falls steeply to a tumble of gritstone boulders. The crags are substantial enough to see considerable rock climbing activity.

Leave by the adjacent stile to return to the moorland side of the wall and continue northwards. Hellifield Crags are the second and more substantial rock outcrops met. Here a steep drop to Waterfall Gill is encountered, but largely avoided, as a sketchy path slopes across to the right. Past the lower boulders of Hellifield Crags it meets the beck without much height loss. Just before reaching the beck, a fine waterfall should be seen lower down. Once across, accompany the crumbling wall scaling the bank. The gradient soon eases and the wall leads to the Rylstone-Bolton Abbey track as it passes through.

Turn right to take advantage of this historic route, immortalised by Wordsworth in his poem The White Doe of Rylstone. The story of the ill-fated Nortons of Rylstone tells of a widow undertaking the trek over the moor to her husband's grave at Bolton Priory: the pet deer that accompanied her continued the journeys even after her death. The track leads onto the heart of

Barden Moor.

the moor, a distinct path featuring a notoriously boggy section now graced with a more durable surface. This remains your way for almost 2 km. During this time you absorb a firmer shooters' track rising from a pair of thatched cabins.

At a guidepost and small cairn, a thin trod breaks off right through a gap in the heather, bound for Embsay. This is your way, faintly across the moor with Embsay Crag gaining in prominence ahead. An old track comes in from a small quarry up to the right, and the way runs on towards the moor edge. Don't drop to the gate, but join the path rising from it to the right, leaving the wall to cross towards Embsay Crag's striking profile. As the ground steepens, the path keeps above a tumble of rocks to the airy summit.

Jutting from its expanse of moorland, Embsay Crag is a notable landmark. Bracken cloaks the lower slopes while heather crowns the top. A tumble of boulders are heaped in wonderful chaos on the southern slopes. This is gritstone country at its best, and the highest rocks are the perfect location for a long break on a warm summer's day, with the reservoir shimmering far below.

The main path can be seen descending the steepest section directly below, but a friendlier way down is to follow a sketchy path along the brink of the rocks to the right. After exchanging heather for bracken another path is met. Turn left along it to join the main path down from the crag. This leads to a footbridge near the head of the reservoir, having earlier passed a left fork which takes in an old quarry. From the footbridge, avoid boggy ground by heading half-right to join a wide track, which followed to the left leads to the stile back off the moor.

On Crookrise Crag Top.

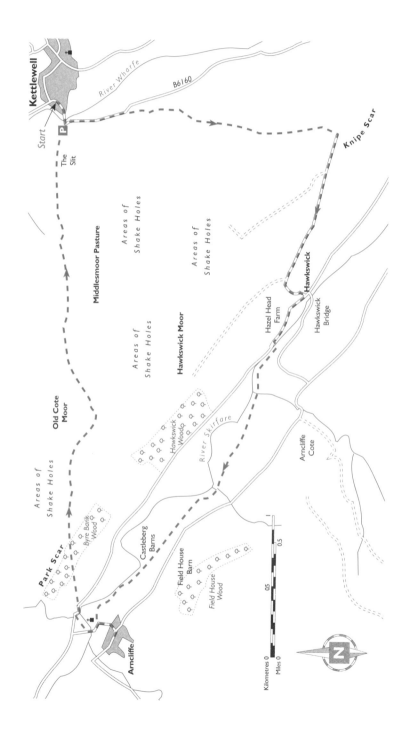

Kettlewell

River Wharfe

B6160

Start

The Slit

Knipe Scar

Middlesmoor Pasture

Areas of Shake Holes

Areas of Shake Holes

Hawkswick Moor

Areas of Shake Holes

Areas of Shake Holes

Old Cote Moor

Hawkswick

Hazel Head Farm

Hawkswick Bridge

Hawkswick Wood

River Skirfare

Areas of Shake Holes

Arncliffe Cote

Byre Bank Wood

Park Scar

Castleberg Barns

Field House Barn

Field House Wood

Arncliffe

Kilometres 0

Miles 0

0.5

0.5

LITTONDALE AND BACK

This walk takes you on an inter-valley crossing on delightful paths, with excellent views. Less than 3 km below Hawkswick, the Skirfare merges with the Wharfe, and during the walk you are treated to unparalleled vistas of substantial lengths of these twin dales immediately above their confluence.

Kettlewell is the hub of the higher reaches of Wharfedale, a junction of roads and a natural halting

INFORMATION

Distance: 10 km
(6 miles).

Start and finish:
Kettlewell. There is a
large car park at the
entrance to the village.

Terrain: Easy walking,
though a steep start.
Trainers are adequate
in dry summer spells.

Public transport:
Kettlewell is served by
bus from Skipton via
Grassington.

Refreshments: Cafes
and pubs in Kettlewell,
pub and tearoom in
Arncliffe, seasonal
refreshments in
Hawkswick.

Kettlewell.

place. It stands on what was a major coaching route to Richmond, and the two inns at the entrance to the village would have serviced weary travellers. The route in question remains a tortuous way over Park Rash and into Coverdale. Shops, tearooms and a third inn add more life to a village being engulfed by holiday homes. The village straddles its own beck which largely drains the slopes of Great Whernside, very much Kettlewell's mountain. These slopes bear the scars of lead mining, an industry replaced by tourism as a partner to farming. Footpaths positively radiate from Kettlewell to all points of the compass, and a richly varied holiday week could be spent here without need of transport.

Leave the village by crossing the road bridge at the entrance and following the road a short distance to a gate and footpath sign pointing up to the right. A good path heads away, bearing right at a fork and rising through trees to a level enclosure. Bearing up to the right beneath a pinewood, a stile is found in the top corner of the field, with another just above. The path then rises through a low scar and continues climbing steadily to a cairn marking the highest point of this crossing of Hawkswick Moor.

Littondale, on descent to Hawkswick.

From the cairn the path undulates across to a stile in the ridge wall. Just beyond is another cairn; from here the path turns sharply right to begin its descent into Littondale. A nice, easy drop concludes by entering Hawkswick, enclosed by walls. Littondale's last village is the only one off the 'main' up-dale road, and remains wonderfully undisturbed. Turn right past the houses to a footbridge, and on crossing it take a stile on the right to accompany Littondale's river, the Skirfare, upstream.

This level walk to Arncliffe is fairly straightforward, with various stiles and gates to point the way. For the most part the river keeps its distance, but it returns for the last kilometre to usher you into the village, a gate by a barn preceding a short drive emerging by the church.

Arncliffe is one of the most attractive yet least spoilt villages in the Dales, and is regarded as the 'capital' of Littondale. A plethora of characterful greystone houses stand back in relaxed manner from a spacious green. The unpretentious Falcon Inn maintains this mood, the only hostelry in the area to serve its ale in that unrivalled fashion, directly from the barrel.

Leave the village green by rejoining the Litton (up-dale) road to St Oswald's church, embowered in trees in a beautiful riverside setting. The solid tower dates back 500 years, while inside is a list of Littondale men who marched off to fight the Scots at Flodden Field in 1513. Cross the bridge over the Skirfare: the house at Bridge End played host to the author Charles Kingsley during his Water Babies period in the 1860s. Born at Holne on Dartmoor, he would have felt at home here.

Once over the bridge, leave the road immediately by a stile on the right to accompany the river downstream, but only as far as another stile onto a narrow road. From the stile opposite, a good path rises diagonally to enter Byre Bank Wood. This ancient pocket of woodland was happily left unfelled due to its steepness, and as a result supports some rare plants. Continue up through the trees, to leave by negotiating the modest limestone cliff of Park Scar at the top.

Maintaining the same course, the path resumes in easier vein. At a gateway in a collapsing wall a short level section precedes the final pull, and at the second of a pair of neighbouring stiles the ridge wall on Old Cote Moor is gained. This is the highest point of the walk. Ahead, Buckden Pike dominates the scene with the uniform looking villages of Buckden and Starbotton at its foot. Great Whernside rises, as ever, above Kettlewell.

Wharfedale above Kettlewell

The descent to Kettlewell commences immediately, the slightly less clear path inclining to the right to eventually locate a stile in a wall descending from the moor top. Continuing down at a similar angle a plateau briefly interrupts the drop before squeezing through the 'Slit', a well used way through a narrow band of limestone. The path then drops down to merge with another before reaching a gate onto the road at the entrance to Kettlewell.

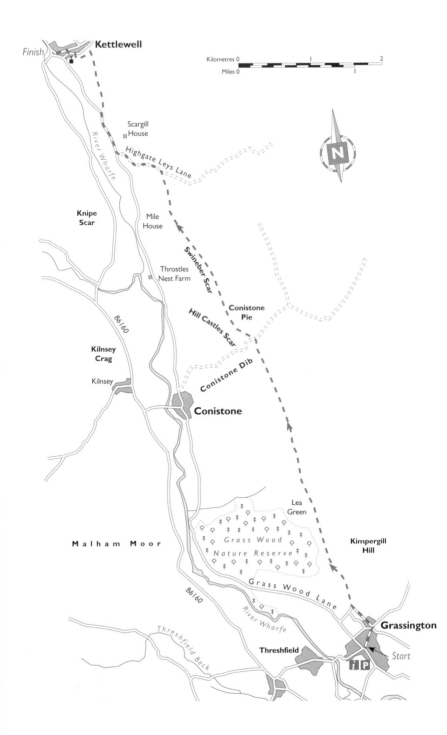

ALONG THE DALES WAY

The Dales Way is a justifiably popular long-distance path, running through the heart of the Yorkshire Dales on its way from Ilkley to Bowness-on-Windermere. For almost half its length it follows the river Wharfe, from bustling Ilkley to windswept Cam Fell, and this sample of the route explores a delectable few miles in Wharfedale. At the

Wharfe at Kettlewell.

The Dales Way approaching Kettlewell.

time of its inception, a lack of riverside paths forced this stage of the Dales Way onto the limestone valley side. Initially a temporary measure, it proved such a successful interlude from the riverbank that it quickly became very much an integral part of the real Dales Way.

INFORMATION

Distance: 11 km (7miles).

Start: Grassington. There is a large National Park car park in the village.

Finish: Kettlewell.

Terrain: Easy walking through fields and along limestone shelfs. There can be muddy sections, though in dry weather light footwear can be adequate.

Public transport: Grassington and Kettlewell are served by bus from Skipton.

Refreshments: Cafes and pubs in Grassington and Kettlewell. Nothing mid-route.

Opening hours: *Upper Wharfedale Folk Museum,* The Square, Grassington: Apr.-Sept. daily 1400– 1630, Oct.-Mar. weekends only 1400– 1630; small admission fee.

A thriving community with a range of facilities, Grassington is undisputed 'capital' of Upper Wharfedale. The cobbled square is the focal point but is really only the shop window: hidden away is enough interest for a day's leisurely exploration. Grassington boasted an 18th century theatre and a lead mining industry of which its nearby moor still bears much evidence. Buildings of character include the Old Hall and the former Town Hall-cum-institute. The folk museum full of artefacts of local interest, is well worth a visit.

Town Head, Grassington.

From the square, head up the main street past the Devonshire Arms to a crossroads, and turn left on Chapel Street. When it eventually turns sharply left, leave it for the farmyard on the right, keeping right of the main buildings and skirting them to arrive at a gate after the last building. Follow the right-hand wall away, and at the end take the middle of three gates. Bear left across the next field to a narrow gap-stile at the end. In the next pasture, curve left to a stile in the far wall, behind which a stile admits onto Lea Green. This great expanse is the site of an ancient British settlement, an extensive field system best appreciated from above (balloon flights sometimes operate from Grassington).

After crossing a wider track, a gentle rise leads up to join another track heading your way. A little further on a sketchy left fork is ignored, and at the brow a near-parallel wall is seen to the right. Your sketchy path remains near it but avoids it until, beyond a limestone pavement, you descend to a stile just before the corner. Just to the right here is an old dewpond, where cattle could slake their thirsts. Head away to skirt a well defined area of outcrops to a gate just beyond, then rise across the bottom of a field to a stile.

Maintain the rise past more outcrops to a solid limekiln constructed of immense stones. Just beyond it a stile is reached, and level pastures precede a pull to the head of Conistone Dib. This spectacular dry valley boasts some memorable limestone features. Your path passes above its tight neck; a minor scramble would be needed to drop down into it. Avoid the stile and take the briefly enclosed way to its right to emerge onto a wide track. Cross over and pass below a scar, above which is a superb limestone pavement. At the end a stile is reached below the knoll of Conistone Pie.

From a distance this inviting little eminence appears man-made, but natural limestone architecture is soon revealed. Crowned by a fine cairn, this sentinel boasts a revealing prospect across Wharfedale's deep trough. Eyes may well first be drawn to the twin-like fork of Littondale striking away. The confluence of its river, the Skirfare, with the Wharfe can be picked out from the path, while close by it is the famous overhang of Kilnsey Crag.

Beyond Conistone Pie the path takes on a level course over stiles in intervening walls. Though the path fades, the route remains obvious below limestone outcrops. When the attendant scar expires, go straight to a stile by a gate into the corner of a plantation. A wide track descends the hillside, passing near Scargill House (a Christian retreat and conference centre) on the right before turning left to emerge onto the back road from Conistone to Kettlewell. The appearance of Scargill House's chapel comes as a shock in this sedate upper dale.

Turn right along the narrow road and after a couple of kinks take a gate on the right at a footpath sign. Head away to a gateway, then turn through it to a gate in the next wall, here commencing a fascinating course taking in about a dozen fields within a kilometre. Though not visible on the ground, the way follows a near-straight wall, twice switching sides before emerging at the head of a narrow green lane on the edge of Kettlewell. Turn down it to a T-junction and then right to emerge onto a back lane. Now go left, passing the Kings Head and then right at the maypole to reach the village centre. Kettlewell is described at the beginning of walk 3.

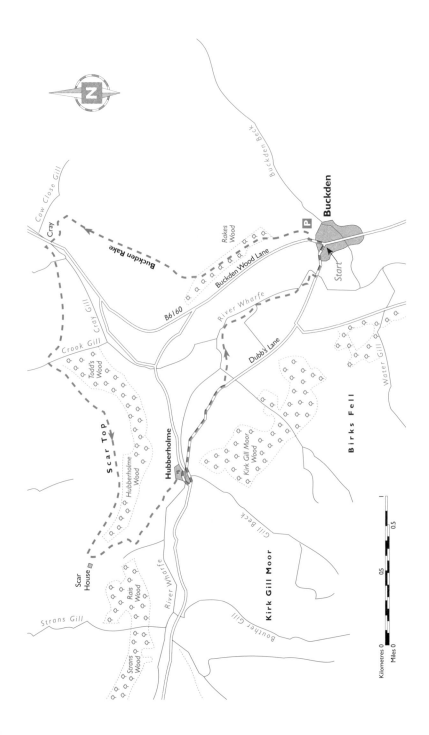

Buckden Beck

Buckden

Cow Close Gill

Cray

Buckden Rake

Rakes Wood

P

Start

Buckden Wood Lane

B6160

River Wharfe

Dubb's Lane

Crook Gill

Cray Gill

Todd's Wood

Scar Top

Hubberholme Wood

Hubberholme

Kirk Gill Moor Wood

Birks Fell

Water Gill

Gill Beck

Scar House

Rais Wood

River Wharfe

Kirk Gill Moor

Bouther Gill

Strans Gill

Strans Wood

Kilometres 0
Miles 0

0.5

0.5

UPPER WHARFEDALE VILLAGES

This is a classic promenade round the valley head, full of variety and interest. Buckden is the first sizeable settlement encountered by the Wharfe, and stands at the meeting place of two high roads from Wensleydale to the north. The good quality B6160 road comes via Cray to take over as the valley road from the narrow, winding strip of tarmac that reaches nearly 600 m on its way over Fleet Moss from Hawes before running through Langstrothdale to Buckden. In medieval times, Buckden was the centre of a vast hunting forest, and its hostelry recalls its former importance in its name. The village stands high above the river on the slopes of Buckden Pike, and swift-flowing Buckden Beck carves a deep defile down from the summit.

Leave the car park not by its exit, but instead by a gate at its northern end, from where a stony track rises gently up Buckden Rake. To the left the upper dale leads to moorland heights, with the Birks Fell ridge behind. At the end of the surround of trees it turns right through a gate to commence a pleasant, level section. On drawing level with the buildings of Cray down to the left, take a gate in the adjacent wall and drop down a steep field to another gate, from where Cray Gill is crossed to join the road right next to the inn.

Situated at over 300 m above sea level, the farming hamlet of Cray is the last outpost of Wharfedale on the high road over to Bishopdale and ultimately Wensleydale. This crossing of the fells is known as the Kidstones Pass, and is the easiest motorable escape out of the valley north of Grassington. Cray's one amenity is the White Lion, an uncomplicated and welcoming hostelry with a flagged floor.

To leave Cray, take the farm track immediately behind the inn and follow it

INFORMATION

Distance: 8 km
(5 miles).

Start and finish: Buckden. There is a large car park in the village.

Terrain: Easy walking on limestone pastures and riverbank. Trainers are adequate in summer.

Public transport: Buckden is served by bus from Skipton via Grassington.

Refreshments: Cafe and pub in Buckden, pubs at Cray and Hubberholme.

Above Buckden Rake, to Cray.

The National Trust,
'Upper Wharfedale'.

up to the left, keeping to the right of the various farm buildings. Having passed through a gate above the last building the way remains level through several fields, becoming indistinct but aiming for a barn just ahead. Go to the left of it, then swing right to a tiny footbridge over Crook Gill.

The walk from Crook Gill to Scar House is along short-cropped turf above a steep drop through ancient woodlands, the scarp being marked by limestone scars and sections of pavement. The slopes to the north rise more steadily to a height of 643 m on the largely unfrequented Yockenthwaite Moor. From Cray to Scar House, you enjoy superlative views down the length of the dale.

From the footbridge swing left to commence a long, easy traverse above the well-defined escarpment cloaked in trees on the left: part-way along, the stately Wharfedale Cairn beckons just up to the right. Sentinel of the upper valley, this solidly built edifice is a notable landmark in the locality, being prominent in many views. All too soon the path arrives just above Scar House. Restored last century, isolated Scar House was the scene of early Quaker gatherings. Turn down between the buildings to accompany the stony access road down the hillside into Hubberholme, emerging alongside the church.

Barely even a hamlet, Hubberholme boasts two famous buildings and a shapely bridge which connects them.

The church of St. Michael is a real gem, its tower showing Norman traces. Its best feature is a 500-year old oak rood loft, one of only two remaining in Yorkshire, while some pews bear the unique and now world famous trademark of the 'Mouseman' workshops. In 1896, Robert Thompson began work at his father's joinery in Kilburn under the North York Moors, and at some uncertain point the celebrated mouse symbol began to appear. Its origins are vague, though a chance remark that his craftsmen were as 'poor as church mice' is put forward. These famous workshops are now a thriving business and tourist attraction, and to this day the mouse symbol adorns all their work.

St. Michael's Church, Hubberholme.

Woodcarving therefore - both ancient and modern - dominates the interior of this highest church in the dale. The famous Yorkshire writer J. B. Priestley chose to be laid to rest here on his death in 1984, such was his love of the place. Outside, meanwhile, the sparkling Wharfe runs almost past its very door. In an idyllic setting across the river is the whitewashed and homely George Inn. Formerly housing the vicar, its flagged floors continued to be the scene of the New Year 'land-letting' when proceeds of a 'poor pasture' go to needy parishioners.

For the final leg of the walk, cross the bridge to the inn and turn left along the road. This narrow section requires a little caution on summer weekends, especially if you've been refreshing yourself in the bar of the George. After about a kilometre, escape by a gate on the left to rejoin the river, which is now accompanied down-dale, soon to reach Buckden Bridge. Join the road to recross the river back into the village.

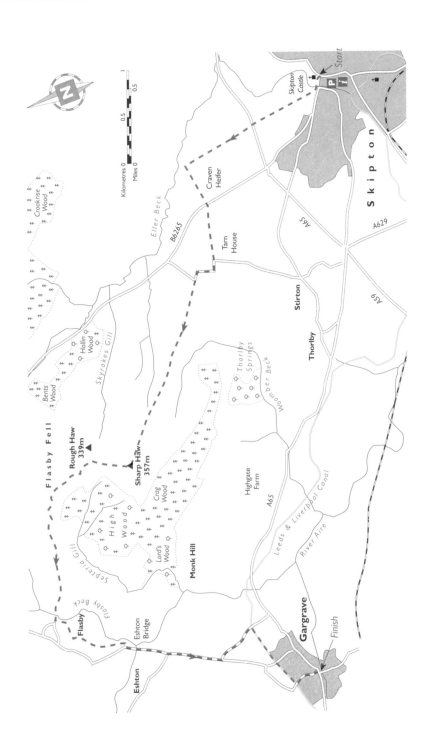

A FLASBY FELL TRAVERSE

Skipton is a fascinating place, much resolve being required to be coaxed away from its many charms. First and foremost are the castle and church, 'cheek by jowl' at the head of the main street, followed by the Craven Museum, the Leeds-Liverpool Canal, and a bustling market four days per week.

First impression of the imposing castle is the magnificent gatehouse, bearing the motto 'Desormais' (henceforth). The castle was founded by the Norman de Romille family, though it is with the Cliffords that Skipton Castle is synonymous. Most of the present building dates from their arrival in 1309. Of their many famous names, best known is the indomitable Lady Anne, last of the Cliffords. During the 17th century she made further additions, and spent much time travelling through the Dales to visit and restore her many other castles.

Lady Anne also helped restore the parish church of the Holy Trinity after damage during the Civil War. Though a splendid building in its own right, once inside it is perhaps inevitable that the Clifford tombs draw attention. The Craven Museum in the Town Hall offers good displays of local interest.

From the roundabout outside the parish church take the Grassington road past the Castle Inn, and over a bridge. Beneath are Eller Beck and a branch of the Leeds-Liverpool Canal. Turn immediately right along a minor road, Chapel Hill, which climbs steeply to end at a gate and stile. Climb straight up the field to a stile at the very top. Close by is a defensive position where a cannon was mounted in Civil War times. Continue in the same direction to the by-pass, which is gained by crossing a parallel farm lane. Cross with care and head directly away again to a stile onto Skipton golf course.

Head straight across, passing a short section of wall to reach the wall ahead, with a small length protruding your way. Take the stile on the left and follow the

INFORMATION

Distance: 11 km (7 miles).

Start: Skipton. There are several car parks in the town.

Finish: Gargrave. Return by bus or train.

Terrain: Open fell sandwiched between field paths. Boots recommended.

Public transport: Skipton is on the Airedale rail line from Leeds/Bradford, and is served by bus from all surrounding towns. Gargrave is the next railway station along the line from Skipton, to which it is also linked by bus.

Refreshments: Refreshments of every kind in Skipton. Pubs, cafe, fish and chips in Gargrave.

Opening hours: *Skipton Castle:* daily 1000–1800, Sundays 1400–1800 (admission fee). *Craven Museum:* Apr-Sep daily except Tue, 1100–1700, Oct-Mar Mon, Wed, Thur, Fri 1400–1700, Sat 1000–1700. *Canal boat trips:* daily (Apr, Oct 1330; May, Jun, Sep 1330 & 1500; Jul-Aug 1130, 1330, 1500, 1630). Charge made.

fence, crossing one final stile before accompanying a fence down onto Brackenley Lane. Turn left to its junction with the Skipton-Grassington road, and cross to a stile opposite. A pub, the Craven Heifer, is just to the left. Aim for a stile at the far side of the field, then head away with a fence which soon falls into disrepair. Continue up the gentle slope to a gate onto a lane just above Tarn House.

Turn right along the lane and at the third sharp bend, take a gate on the left to follow a gently rising track. After two more gates, open country is entered. When the accompanying wall breaks off to the left, leave the track by bearing off to the right. On climbing the slope a

faint path materialises, and improves as the top of Sharp Haw is neared and the going steepens a little. An old iron stile in the wall across the top admits to the Ordnance Survey column on Sharp Haw's airy summit. At a modest 357 m, Sharp Haw is the shapely summit of Flasby Fell, the triangle of upland between Skipton, Gargrave and Rylstone: it is, quite simply, a grand place to be.

Cracoe Fell from Sharp Haw.

Neighbouring Rough Haw, a less distinctive hill, sits across the depression to the north. Follow the path along the short ridge for a few yards, where it drops to the right to a gateway in the wall. The path heads straight down the slope and across the depression to a gate and stile. Directly in front now are the short, steep slopes of Rough Haw. The main path, however, heads along to the left.

A fork is quickly reached: while a more obvious branch descends left towards the top corner of a wood, the bridleway forges straight on, a clear path through the bracken-covered flanks of Rough Haw. Further on it too swings down to the left, out of the bracken now and with a wall just beyond. Descend the near side of the wall, swinging left near a corner to drop down alongside Septeria Gill to a gate in the very bottom corner, where the direct path is met. Continue along the edge of the field to another gate, from where an enclosed track winds down to the yard of Flasby Hall Farm. Founded by the Danes over a thousand years ago, Flasby consists of a few scattered houses and farms.

Cross the bridge over the beck and up the lane. At the first chance go left along a drive serving a few houses. Before the gate at the end take a stile on the right, up a few steps to the next stile then up the field-side with a fence. From the stile at the top go left to the corner just in front. There is a good prospect of Flasby Hall just down to the left. Cross another stile and then follow a fence all the way along to the narrowing end alongside a wood. Here an enclosed path curves up onto a road. Go left to drop down to Eshton Bridge. Go left to the junction with the Malham road, then on towards Gargrave.

The canal at Skipton.

At the next junction go left on a narrow lane leading to Ray Bridge over the canal. Steps on the right gives access to the towpath. The Leeds to Liverpool Canal was completed in 1816, though by 1777 this easternmost section was already in operation. It runs for 127¼ miles (milestones along its course confirm this precise figure!) between the two great cities, and remains entirely navigable. Its builders exploited the Aire Gap to take this northernmost and longest of the trans-Pennine canals across the country's backbone.

A vast network of locks was necessary to lift the waterway through the hills without the need for major tunnels. Though built to serve – as well it did – the commerce of the many towns along its route, sadly its working lifespan was short. The arrival of the far more efficient railways quickly spelt the death knell, though today it is a growing leisure amenity. At Skipton boat trips are available (see Information section for times) on a 200-year-old boat.

Gargrave.

Leave the towpath at the second road crossing, at Higherland Lock, and go left down the road into the centre of Gargrave to end the walk.

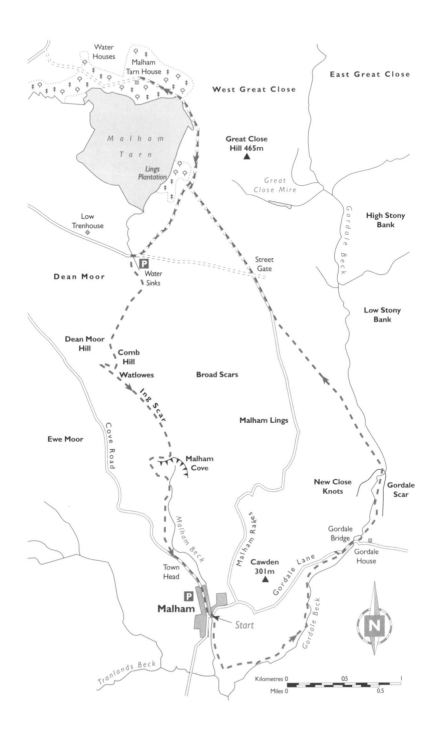

Water
Houses

Malham
Tarn House

West Great Close

East Great Close

*Malham
Tarn*

**Great Close
Hill 465m** ▲

*Great
Close Mire*

*Lings
Plantation*

Low
Trenhouse

G o r d a l e   B e c k

**High Stony
Bank**

🅿
*Water
Sinks*

Street
Gate

Dean Moor

**Low Stony
Bank**

**Dean Moor
Hill**

**Comb
Hill**

Watlowes

Broad Scars

Ing Scar

Malham Lings

Ewe Moor

Cove Road

Malham
Cove

**New Close
Knots**

**Gordale
Scar**

Malham Beck

Malham Rakes

Gordale
Bridge

Gordale
House

Town
Head

**Cawden
301m** ▲

Gordale Lane

Gordale Beck

🅿
Malham

→ *Start*

N

Tranlands Beck

Kilometres 0   0.5   1
Miles 0   0.5

MASTERPIECES OF MALHAM

This mainly easy walk through stunning limestone scenery is a must for all Dales visitors. At Gordale Scar you have to tackle a short climb on rock – this is a fairly simple task with ample hand-holds, but may be outside the scope of less agile walkers. It is beyond all non-amphibious walkers after heavy rain.

Though visitors are drawn to Malham for its scenic surrounds, the village is attractive in its own right. Many cottages date from the 17th and early 18th centuries, while in earlier times the land was shared between Bolton Priory and Fountains Abbey, and reminders of their granges are found in two of the bridges over Malham Beck. Monk Bridge was once a packhorse bridge, now widened into a road bridge, while Prior Moon's Bridge is one of several clapper bridges. Two inns are centrally placed along with two modern purpose-built structures, a youth hostel and a National Park Centre.

INFORMATION

Distance: 12 km (7 miles).

Start and finish: Malham. There is a large car park at the entrance to the village.

Terrain: Exceptionally easy walking on limestone pastures. Boots recommended in view of several rougher sections, but trainers may be adequate in summer, if you're happy with the lack of underfoot support over rough ground.

Public transport: Malham is served by infrequent bus from Skipton.

Refreshments: Cafes and pubs in Malham; possibly an ice cream van on the road near Malham Tarn.

Opening hours: The National Park Centre has a wide range of information and publications available, and a display of local features of interest (open daily Easter–Oct 1000–1600, and some winter weekends).

Above Malham Cove.

From the car park head into the village, crossing the beck by a footbridge by the forge and doubling back downstream. From a gate a broad path heads across the fields. At a kissing-gate the path swings left to a barn, crosses to the left of the wall and continues in the same direction. The outer portals of Gordale await, but as yet reveal nothing of the grandeur to come. Malham Cove, however, already asserts itself behind the village.

Gordale Beck is soon joined and followed upstream. On entering woodland, the enchanting Janet's Foss is quickly reached. Legend has it that Janet, queen of the local fairies, had a cave behind the falls. What is more certain is that the wood provides a rich habitat for a wide variety of flora and fauna. Here the path breaks off left onto the road. Turn right, crossing the beck and arriving at a gate on the left just before Gordale House. A well trodden path crosses the pasture to the impending cliffs of Gordale Scar, which converge as you enter the dark confines.

In Gordale Scar.

Gordale Scar is the most awe-inspiring single feature in the Dales. Unlike the Cove, which bares all on first sighting, the Scar waits for you to turn the final corner before impressing you to the full. Once in its dark confines the grandeur of the overhanging cliffs can be too daunting to fully appreciate the waterfalls: the upper one spills in spectacular fashion through a window in the rock.

Escape by negotiating the rock to the left of the lower falls. This straightforward scramble with ample hand-holds nevertheless demands care. Above it, the stony path clings to the left side of the gorge, passing the upper fall and breaking out into green pastures. Running straight ahead is the upper Gordale Valley. Beyond a stile the path becomes sketchy, but the way remains fairly obvious. A long, low line of limestone outcrops deflects the path left, and a long trek ensues to a stile onto the road to

Malham Tarn. Follow this right, and at a minor crossroads keep straight on along the drive to Malham Tarn House.

A gate leads into the grounds, now in the hands of the National Trust (admission is free to the grounds, though notices define which sections can be explored off the public footpath). Advance as far as you wish: the drive runs closer to the shore as it approaches the woods enclosing the house itself. At 375 m above sea-level, Malham Tarn is an extensive sheet of water, its existence being due to a layer of silurian slate. The surrounding wetlands, woodland and limestone pavement all contribute to its status as a National Nature Reserve.

Back at the gate, bear right off the drive and over the brow of the open moor on a fainter green way, rejoining the road at Water Sinks Gate. Pass through, take a gate on the left and follow the wall to Water Sinks. Here the tarn's outflow disappears deep into the ground, only returning to the surface 3 km away at Aire Head Springs below the village. Beyond it, the path becomes clearer as limestone surroundings return.

Yet another grand moment awaits as you arrive at the head of Watlowes, a dry valley. Faced with an impasse, the path runs along a terrace to the right, then descends to the green and stony floor. Simply trace this along to arrive at the extensive pavement above Malham Cove. Though fascinating to tread, take great care as the deep grikes in between have little sympathy with your ankles. The great limestone cliff of Malham Cove rises 100 m from the valley floor, and this approach from above is unquestionably the most dramatic.

Highfolds Scar from Malham Tarn.

Turn right across the pavement to a set of wall-stiles from where a path descends to the foot of the Cove. Before leaving, a path leads temptingly to the very foot of the cliffs. Issuing from the base is Malham Beck, which also sank on the moor. To finish, a well tramped path heads downstream through the fields to emerge onto the road just short of the village.

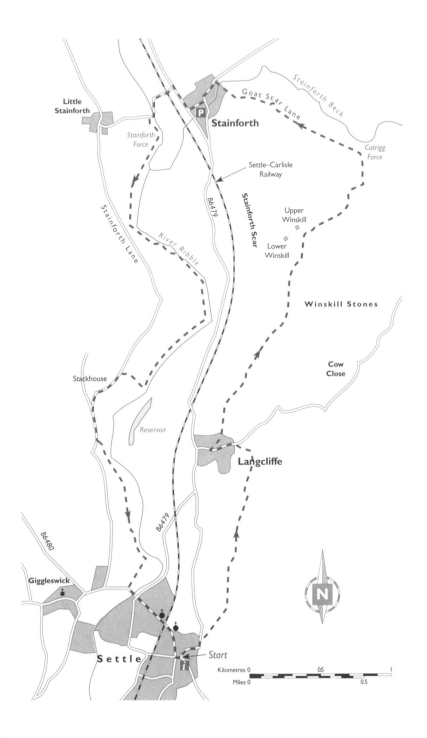

Little
Stainforth

Stainforth Force

Goat Scar Lane

Stainforth Beck

P

Stainforth

Catrigg Force

Settle–Carlisle
Railway

B6479

Stainforth Lane

River Ribble

Stainforth Scar

Upper
Winskill

Lower
Winskill

Winskill Stones

**Cow
Close**

Stackhouse

Reservoir

Langcliffe

B6479

B6480

Giggleswick

N

S e t t l e

Start

i

Kilometres 0   0.5   1
Miles 0   0.5

LIMESTONE RIBBLESDALE

This is a leisurely limestone ramble, with a lovely riverside stretch as the icing on the cake.

Settle is a bustling little town which acts as an important focal point for Upper Ribblesdale, and a long-established halting place for those bound further afield. Market days present the liveliest scene, when the small square is awash with colour. The town boasts numerous old buildings, some hidden and others very much on display. Facing the square is the historic row known as the Shambles, with shops peeping from behind archways. Nearby is the Folly, a rambling 17th century house with an intricate facade. Also facing the square is a former inn, 'the Naked Man', its appropriate carved sign of 1633 being a source of some humour. The Museum of North Craven Life gives a rewarding insight into the district's past, while the limestone cliff of Castleberg provides a dramatic bird's-eye view of the town today.

Leave the market place by Constitution Hill, left of the Shambles. The road goes left after a steep climb, and almost at once is abandoned in favour of the rougher Banks Lane to the right. On emerging to cross a field bottom it is briefly enclosed again before heading along to a stile. Continue with another wall before dropping left to emerge onto the road out of Langcliffe. Turn into this lovely village which is scattered beyond the extensive green. By the phone box look for a tablet on a house wall depicting the Naked Woman, and modestly dated 1660. Once an inn, it was a close friend of Settle's more famous Naked Man.

The point of departure is the second lane on the right on entering the village, after the school. Go straight over an early crossroads to follow a splendid green lane all the way to its demise. Opt for the right-hand gate to run along the field top, and from the gate at the far end a way climbs steeply above the lip of an old

INFORMATION

Distance: 10 km (6 miles).

Start and finish: Settle. There are several car parks in the town.

Terrain: Largely easy walking through limestone pastures. Boots recommended in other than dry, summery conditions.

Public transport: Settle is served by bus from Skipton and Ingleton, and has a station on the Settle-Carlisle Railway.

Refreshments: Cafes and pubs in Settle, shop in Langcliffe, pub at Stainforth.

Opening hours: *The Museum of North Craven Life:* Easter-Jun Sat, Sun & Bank Holidays 1400–1700, Jul-Sep Tue-Sat & Bank Holidays 1400–1700; small admission charge).

quarry. A small gate in the top corner is the key to continuing up the next smaller enclosure, which is left by a stile right of a walled track heading left. A field is crossed to empty onto Lower Winskill's drive, turning right to arrive at the entrance to Upper Winskill Farm.

Your route crosses straight over the track directly ahead, which peters out shortly after a stile. Another stile is soon seen ahead, and from it the descent to Catrigg Force can be made. Its location is in no doubt, being enshrouded in trees at the bottom of the field. A pair of neighbouring stiles lead to the top of the waterfall, where with great care you can peer down to

Stainforth Force.

the bottom. The conventional view of this waterfall as lovely as any in the Dales can be sampled by entering the trees on the left to descend a good path to the foot of the ravine. The rough lane alongside is Goat Scar Lane, which leads all the way down to Stainforth.

Stainforth is a sizeable village stood high above and well back from the Ribble. Centrally located is the Craven Heifer, a multi-roomed inn sporting a popular local name. A particularly pleasing corner can be found where stepping stones cross the beck by a small green. Stainforth's better known features, however, are located outside the village, including an 18th century mansion which is currently a youth hostel.

From the pub, cross the bridge and turn left to meet the valley road alongside the car park. Turn right along it, leaving almost immediately by a narrow road to the left. Bridging the railway, it descends to cross the graceful 17th century Stainforth Bridge, built to serve the York-Lancaster packhorse trade. Immediately over, take a stile on the left and turn downstream to Stainforth Force. The combination of bridge, riverbank, waterfall and adjacent caravan site make this a place of popular resort. The falls are indeed idyllically sited, and are a rare burst of activity for the Ribble.

Resume downstream, shortly after which the path briefly leaves the river and is routed across the field to the wooded bank ahead. From here on it remains in

Catrigg Force.

close company, passing a paper mill and some pleasant woodland to reach the footbridge at the Locks, an attractive scene. Don't use the bridge other than as a viewpoint, but turn up the green lane to the right. This emerges onto Stackhouse Lane. Go left along it past the exclusive hamlet of Stackhouse and continue just as far as a stile on the left.

Cross to the field corner and follow a wooded bank high above the river. Opposite is the Langcliffe paper mill. At the end a fine stile sends the path across a field, going left at the end to meet the river. An enclosed path then runs between sports fields to join the road at Settle Bridge. Cross the Ribble to re-enter the town, ending your walk under the railway viaduct.

Langcliffe.

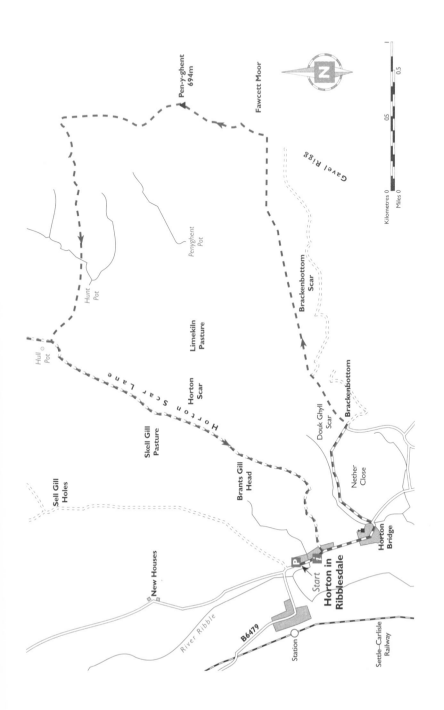

PENYGHENT, LION OF RIBBLESDALE

This walk follows the classic ascent route of the easiest of the Three Peaks. Evidence of its popularity is with you throughout much of the walk, but it remains a grand excursion. To the few who might be unaware, the Three Peaks of Yorkshire are Whernside, Ingleborough and Penyghent, all grouped around the headwaters of the river Ribble. In 1887, a pair of Giggleswick schoolmasters chose to embrace all three within a day's walk, and so a legend was born. Everyone with a pair of boots – and many without – latched onto the challenge of completing the three ascents in a continuous walk within a 12-hour time limit. They came in droves: sponsored walkers, challenge walkers, and then the crazy element as people manhandled vehicles and everything but the kitchen sink over these bemused and battered hills.

The inevitable result was erosion on a grand scale: the three hills would have had enough trouble coping with the feet of casual walkers, but the triple whammy was more than the fragile peaty sections of the landscape could handle. Exactly a century after the schoolmasters' celebrated walk, the Yorkshire Dales National Park set about a programme of path restoration which was to prove a far greater, and more expensive, task than envisaged. Just about every type of pathwork has been tried, varying with the type of terrain. Earliest efforts saw wooden duckboards appearing: temporarily effective but clearly not ideal. Since then we have seen pitched stone paths and hard, crushed limestone bases, and witnessed increasing success in many parts of the district.

The ancient method of laying a 'floating' path has invoked a modern equivalent, a durable plastic matting on which a stone path can be floated. Re-seeding with stronger vegetation, and experimentation with various soil enriching fertilisers and lime have been used with further success. The great learning process in this vast and unique 'outdoor laboratory' continues, and one happy result is that much new-found knowledge has been passed on to help similar problem areas elsewhere. It is fair to say that today, for the most part, our steps have little impact as the paths are largely of such a durable nature: nevertheless, it is wise to remain on the paths and thus not create further problems to be solved.

Horton in Ribblesdale is the highest village in a valley which ends in the Irish Sea beyond Preston, and is very much the centre of Three Peaks country. It has little intrinsic charm, being a curious mixture of dwellings strung along the road, and overlooked by a horrendous quarry. Several datestones adorn cottage lintels dating back to the late 17th century. Horton's real attraction is its location, as the sight of countless boots being pulled on in its car park will testify: the place has a true walkers' atmosphere.

A renowned cafe caters for the weary, while inns are found at either end of the street. The Crown has two arched bridges outside, while the Golden Lion faces St Oswald's church: this displays a Norman doorway and arcades in the nave. The solid-looking 15th century tower has leanings towards Pisa: not quite so emphatic, perhaps, but lean to the south it certainly does. The

St. Oswalds, Horton.

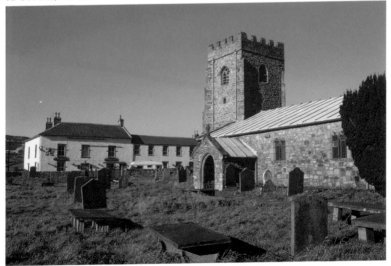

pub, meanwhile, re-opened in 1988 after an 18-year dry spell when it functioned as an outdoor education centre.

From the village centre, head down the road to the church at the southern end, and just over the beck turn up the side road. This runs past the school and around to Brackenbottom. En route, look over to the left to see the highly prominent Douk Gill Head. This is the resurgence of the waters entering the mighty chasm of Hull Pot, amongst others. Brackenbottom is a farming hamlet that incorporates a caving club base.

Immediately before the buildings, enter a small enclosure on the left, cross it and then head up the field-side. The clear route of ascent is entirely uncomplicated as it follows a wall up the slopes of the fell. Ahead, Penyghent's 'crouching lion' impression makes an inspirational objective. Eventually, after one or two ups and downs, you gain the foot of its south ridge proper, and earn views eastwards to Fountains Fell.

Over the stile, turn left up the wall-side for the final push, a section that comprises two distinct halves as you tackle first a limestone band, then clamber through a boulderfield to engage the upper, gritstone band. Beyond that you are virtually on the top, and a simple stroll leads up to the Ordnance Survey column and cairns.

A sturdy wall traverses the felltop, and offers itself as a priceless shelter when the elements are at their wildest: indeed, Penyghent actually means 'hill of the winds'. Its close ally Ingleborough dominates the view, which covers much of the Yorkshire Dales and places beyond, most notably the rolling moors of Bowland beyond the Ribble Valley. Though lowest of the Three Peaks, it is only Penyghent that draws climbers to its gritstone buttresses, and, for better or worse, only Penyghent attracts walkers attempting the Pennine Way.

Penyghent ascent.

Leave by crossing the stile and heading along the broad path slanting away. This quickly reaches a well defined edge above gritstone outcrops, and then deflects northwards to work down to the limestone band once again. A path junction is a major turning point. The traditional 'Three Peaks' route slants off down the fellside, but yours begins the unmistakable direct descent on one of the earlier sections of 'made' paths on the Three Peaks. First, however, a look along to the right reveals the spectacular finger of rock known as Penyghent Pinnacle. This limestone spire is only appreciated at close quarters, for otherwise its detachment from the line of crags is not seen.

Your path, meanwhile, works straight down the fell. Ahead, the gaping hole of Hull Pot waits to swallow up the skies, such is its girth. The path descends to the head of Horton Scar Lane. Just before it, the sinister slit of Hunt Pot can be located just off the path. Caution is urged if attempting to peer in here, for the depth is thought to be around 60m. Before turning down the lane, go right for five level minutes along the broad track to arrive at Hull Pot. This magnificent chasm is a remarkable contrast to Hunt Pot, an almighty hole in the heart of the moor. Roughly 100 m long and 20 m wide, it is seen at its finest when a waterfall plunges over its rim. In normal conditions the stream will have sunk below ground before getting this far.

Back at the lane head, simply follow this rough, walled track all the way down to the village, enjoying views across to Penyghent's familiar profile, and over the valley too. The lane emerges in the village centre, where you can take your choice of refreshments to enjoy while you reflect on the grand outing just completed.

Penyghent from Dale Head

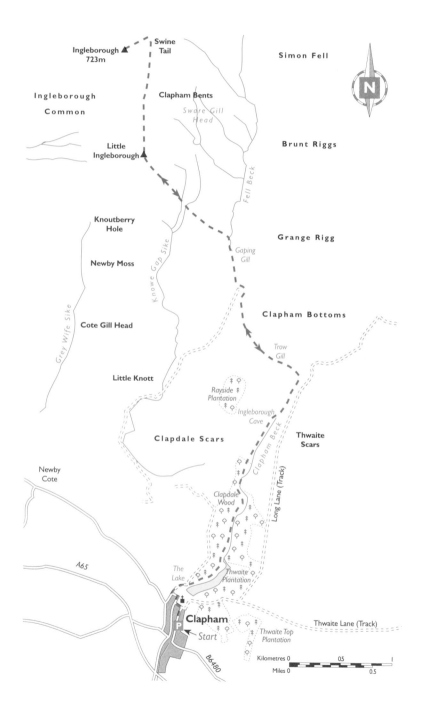

Ingleborough
723m

Swine
Tail

Simon Fell

Ingleborough
Common

Clapham Bents

Sware Gill
Head

Brunt Riggs

Little
Ingleborough

Knoutberry
Hole

Grange Rigg

Gaping
Gill

Newby Moss

Clapham Bottoms

Cote Gill Head

Little Knott

Trow
Gill

Rayside
Plantation

Ingleborough
Cave

Clapdale Scars

Thwaite
Scars

Newby
Cote

Clapdale
Wood

The
Lake

Thwaite
Plantation

Clapham

Start

Thwaite Lane (Track)

Thwaite Top
Plantation

Kilometres 0   0.5   1
Miles 0   0.5

GAPING GILL AND INGLEBOROUGH

Clapham is a beautiful village in a setting to match. Sturdy bridges cross tree-lined Clapham Beck and cosy cottages abound. The National Park Centre is based in the old manor house, which bears a lintel dated 1705: a wide range of information and publications are available, with a

Clapham.

display on features of particular local interest. For many decades Clapham provided the cottage home for that revered Yorkshire magazine, the 'Dalesman'. Near the church with its 15th century tower is Ingleborough Hall, home of the Farrer family and now an outdoor centre. A century ago Reginald Farrer brought exotic plants back from his travels to plant in the grounds of the hall.

From the car park cross the road to a footbridge and take the road up to the right. As it turns left, a gate on the right leads to the cottage where entry is gained to

INFORMATION

Distance: 14 km (9 miles).

Start and finish: Clapham. There is a large car park in the village.

Terrain: A strenuous walk to the second highest Dales mountain. Beyond Trow Gill the easy track becomes a rugged moorland path, and despite much restoration work, there are some rough and boggy sections. Boots are essential, as are waterproofs, spare clothes, food and drink. In winter conditions this can be a serious undertaking. Ordnance Survey 1:25,000 Outdoor Leisure Map 2 (Yorkshire Dales, Western area) is recommended.

Public transport: Clapham is served by Settle-Ingleton buses, and also has a station on the Leeds-Morecambe line.

Refreshments: Cafes and pub in Clapham. Light refreshments at Ingleborough Cave. If you intend to go all the way to Ingleborough's summit, then it is important you have adequate food and drink, at any time of year.

Opening hours: *Ingleborough Cave:* open daily Mar-Oct 1000-1600, Nov-Feb weekends only 1000-1600; admission fee. This is a show cave with guided tours. *National Park Centre:* open daily Easter-Oct 1000-1600, and some winter weekends.

Note: A small admission fee is payable to enter the private Ingleborough estate grounds.

Ingleborough above Thornton.

the private grounds (very small admission fee). A wide track goes right of the cottage and zigzags up to the foot of the lake. The broad carriageway of Clapdale Drive is followed the length of the grounds. Encountered en route is the Grotto, a useful shelter in rain, but the water that will be appreciated is the artificial lake locked in glorious woodland.

At the end you emerge into the open air of Clapdale to trace the beck to Ingleborough Cave, a show cave with guided tours. A fascinating underground world awaits, where concrete paths take you deep into the bowels of Ingleborough. Imaginative floodlighting allows you to savour the many delights, featuring outstanding cave formations overlooking deep pools and subterranean streams. Consider enjoying this experience on the return, when better aware of the time available. Just yards past it a stone arched bridge crosses the beck within a few metres of its birth. On the left is Beck Head, from where the waters gush. The stream last saw daylight as Fell Beck, plunging into Gaping Gill. A connection by cavers was established in the 1980s.

Beyond here, a corner is rounded to climb through the overhanging ravine of Trow Gill, a former cave that is now a dry valley. Emerging onto open moor the path accompanies a wall, crossing it at the second stile. Just behind is Bar Pot, and a few minutes further the path leads a little roughly (and moistly) to the unmistakable hollow of Gaping Gill.

Gaping Gill is the most famous hole in the Dales. On the open moor in the lap of Ingleborough, this mighty chasm cannot fail to impress. The innocuous stream of Fell Beck suddenly falls an unbroken 100 m from the unfenced lip to the floor of a chamber said to be of sufficient size to hold York Minster. This is no place for skylarking or unrestrained children. On the main bank holiday weekends, caving clubs set up a chair and winch to lower people down. If not charged for the descent, you'll have to pay to return to the surface! Several miles of passages radiate from the main chamber, and the course of Fell Beck finally returns to daylight as Clapham Beck, as already witnessed.

For the well prepared, Gaping Gill is a natural springboard for the ascent of Ingleborough. A path cuts back across the moor, rejoining the direct path to face the stiff pull up the shoulder of Little Ingleborough. Once gained the hard work is done, and the restored path past an old sheepfold culminates in a gentle slant up onto the summit plateau. The highest point is found on the opposite side.

The top boasts much of interest: a wind shelter with seating and view indicator; an Ordnance Survey column; a massive cairn; and a great pile of stones nearer the Ingleton edge. The latter item is the ruin of a 'hospice' erected in 1830 and largely destroyed on the spot due to the drunken revelries of those celebrating its construction. Crumbling walls around the rim of the plateau are the remains of an Iron age hillfort. As a viewpoint Ingleborough warrants superlatives, its position as a cornerstone of the Dales guaranteeing variety of scenery. 'Inland' is a full skyline of rolling tops slotted in between colleagues Penyghent and Whernside; far to the west are the mountains of Lakeland; southwards are the Bowland moors, while Morecambe Bay glistens beyond Arnside Knott.

The return route follows the outward one: care is need in leaving the plateau in poor conditions, for the bare, stony top holds little in the way of paths, and the beginning of the Clapham path is not obvious until you are upon it. If time permits, then Ingleborough Cave presents a welcome deviation with the knowledge that the village is only half an hour's good stride further.

North from Ingleborough.

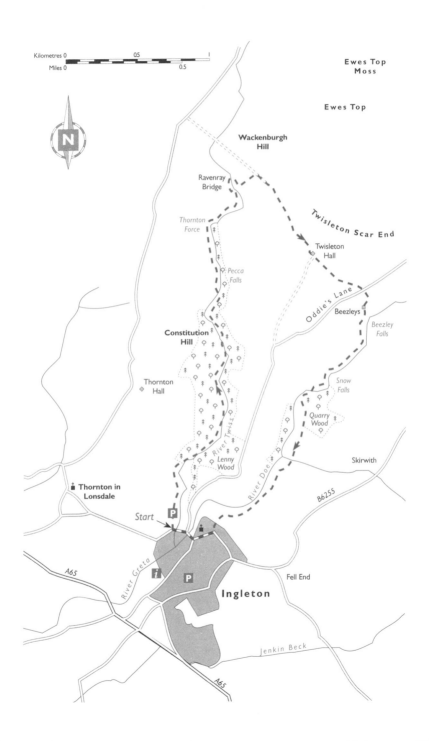

Kilometres 0   0.5   1
Miles 0   0.5

N

Ewes Top Moss

Ewes Top

Wackenburgh Hill

Ravenray Bridge

Thornton Force

Twisleton Scar End

Twisleton Hall

Pecca Falls

Beezleys

Beezley Falls

Oddie's Lane

Constitution Hill

Thornton Hall

Snow Falls

Quarry Wood

River Twiss

Skirwith

Lenny Wood

River Doe

B6255

⚑ **Thornton in Lonsdale**

Start

🅿

Ingleton

Fell End

River Greta

ℹ

🅿

A65

Jenkin Beck

A65

THE WATERFALLS WALK

Universally known as the Waterfalls Walk, this is a hugely popular excursion, and no wonder! Operated by the 'Ingleton Scenery Company', it has attracted visitors for over a century, and more so than any other in this book, it is worth savouring in one of the winter months when free of jostling crowds. Don't come following a prolonged drought. Budding geologists will have the time of their lives. A detailed trail leaflet can be purchased at the ticket kiosk.

A principal reason for this wonderful scenery is the Craven Fault, which reveals itself on several occasions. The North Craven Fault is witnessed at Pecca Quarries, while the South Craven Fault is seen at its most impressive at Meal Bank, on emerging from the eastern glen. The waterfalls themselves have been formed by the action of the fast flowing streams, which have worked through the porous limestone and down to harder rocks below. The departure of the last Ice Age, meanwhile, a mere few thousand years ago, heralded the beginnings of the gorges and subsequently forming waterfalls. Whatever your interpretation, you cannot fail to be impressed once you get walking.

The names of the different watercourses have caused confusion over the years. The outward valley is that of the Twiss, the return one that of the Doe. In Ingleton itself, just below the start, in fact, they merge to form the Greta. Upstream, meanwhile, the Twiss begins life as Kingsdale Beck, and the Doe starts out as Chapel Beck. The mighty wedge of Whernside's southern ridge divides them.

Ingleton is famed as the centre for Yorkshire's limestone country, and is certainly a good base for exploring the fells, scars, caves and valleys of the area. The roadside signs proclaiming 'Beauty Spot of the North' may raise the odd smile, but only from blinkered travellers on the busy A65 which avoids the

INFORMATION

Distance: 7 km (4½ miles).

Start and finish: Ingleton. Start from the Falls car park, reached by descending the steep road by the church.

Refreshments: Cafes and pubs in Ingleton, seasonal refreshments along the route.

Terrain: The paths are well maintained everywhere – justifying the charge – but care is still needed when wet leaves carpet the ground. Be also aware that for a low level walk, there is a fair amount of 'up and down' work. Boots are recommended.

Public transport: Ingleton is served by buses from Kirkby Lonsdale and Settle.

Opening hours: The Waterfalls Walk is open daily throughout the year 0900–1630 (admission fee payable). Single visitors and couples will find it more cost effective to park elsewhere and enter as a pedestrian!

village centre and its nearby attractions. A dominant feature of the village centre is a redundant viaduct. At one time people could board at Ingleton station and cross the viaduct to Thornton in Lonsdale station for a penny (old money!). The railway reached Ingleton in 1849, but for its first 11 years was operated as a local enterprise only, being pulled by horses between here and Clapham.

In 1861 a through service opened up the Lune Valley, running north to meet the Lancaster-Carlisle line at Lowgill, short of Tebay. Sadly the Clapham-Lowgill section met its demise several decades ago. Also prominent is the parish church, and there are numerous interesting little corners. The youth hostel is centrally situated. The 'beauty' of Ingleton, however, is surely its location, and the many charms of this walk will further confirm Ingleton's appeal as a very special one.

Few directions are needed as the paths are very clear throughout, and the way obvious. Alongside the ticket kiosk stand the forlorn remains of a former railway line that ran from Meal Bank Quarry across the river (seen on the return) to join the then main line. From the car park, the path heads up the valley of the Twiss, and of immediate interest is an arched tree into which thousands of pennies have been wedged. Passing through Swilla Glen, the charms are many, yet you haven't even seen a waterfall so far! This is soon remedied as the river is re-crossed to witness Pecca Falls thundering over a drop of 30 m through the trees. On the left here are the sizeable remains of old slate quarries.

Pecca Falls.

A steep climb winds up past the clear leap of Hollybush Spout and out into open country. A renowned refreshment hut is passed to reach the walk's highlight, the 14 m drop of Thornton Force. Nobody can pass through here without taking a break, and indeed most visitors make this their picnic location, scattered around the grassy walled amphitheatre. An abundance of apoplectic geologists and bemused students clearly suggests there is something special about it. Even to the untrained eye the environs of the

Thornton Force.

waterfall are intriguing as horizontally bedded limestone rests on vertical beds of slates. In the space of a few metres in height, millions upon millions of years are spanned: quite incomprehensible to envisage in the context of our own short timespan.

Above Thornton Force the path climbs around Raven Ray to reveal the flat valley floor of Kingsdale. In the last Ice Age boulder clay deposited here formed Raven Ray, a classic example of a moraine which dammed Kingsdale to create a glacial lake. Another bridge takes the path up onto the waiting Twisleton Lane, where an ice cream van may well be plying its trade. Turn right along its green course to Twisleton Hall, and keep left of the buildings, using two stiles and a track which descends to a quiet road, Oddie's Lane. There are some fine views over to the majestic profile of Ingleborough from this upper section of the walk, which is very much its mid point.

Pecca Twin Falls.

Cross straight over to Beezleys Farm, passing between the buildings to a gate on the left. Drop down to Beezley Falls and follow the river Doe back. Features along the way include a precariously sited viewing platform above Baxengill Gorge; the lovely Snow Falls; and this time only one crossing of the beck. Emergence from the trees is high above the river at Cat Leap Fall. The path runs on to a road end to re-enter the village. The final section enjoys a striking prospect of the tilted rock strata in the old quarry at Meal Bank, opposite.

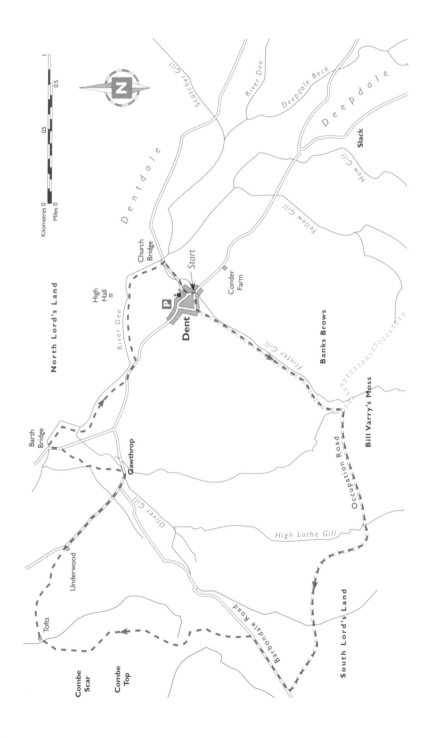

TIMELESS DENTDALE

Beckside and fellside walking combine on this undemanding outing to give delightful close-hand and majestic distant views.

Dent is only a village in size, but is still known as Dent Town in recognition of its once greater importance. Today it is an unhurried backwater midway along its own valley: the only roads in and out are narrow, minor ones, a factor which has helped preserve Dent's character. Retained are some cobbled streets lined with neat cottages, a few shops, a pair of inns and a lovely church.

St. Andrew's occupies an influential position in the heart of the village, and its size confirms the once greater importance of Dent. It dates in part from the 15th century, though the tower dates only from the late 18th century. The floor of the chancel is Dent marble, a locally quarried type of limestone. Both the Sun Inn and the George & Dragon serve ale brewed just up the road in this very dale: support a local industry and savour an excellent product at the same time!

By the side of the main street is a huge block of Shap granite in use as a drinking fountain, and carved with the name Adam Sedgwick. Born here in 1785, he

INFORMATION

Distance: 9 km (6 miles).

Start and finish: Dent. There is a large car park in the village.

Terrain: Easy walking on field paths and tracks. Trainers are adequate in summer.

Public transport: Dent is served by very occasional (school) bus from Sedbergh. Dent station, on the Settle-Carlisle Railway, is 7 km (4 miles) distant!

Refreshments: Cafe and pubs in Dent, seasonal refreshments in Gawthrop.

Dent Town.

spent over 50 years as Professor of Geology at Cambridge. One of the earliest and best in his field, he did much pioneering research into the fascinating geology of his own back yard, notably his identification of the important Dent Fault. Despite the standards and the position he achieved, he returned regularly to his humble beginnings, where indeed much of his (earlier) work was done. A geological trail in the adjacent valley of Garsdale was opened in 1985 to commemorate this local man who went to the very top of his profession.

From the car park, cross the road and take the road rising past the memorial hall. A delightful grouping of cottages marks the start of Flinter Gill, with an old Methodist chapel on the left. The narrow road becomes a stony track to start climbing above the beck. In its enchanting setting, Flinter Gill tumbles over a series of rock ledges, though after a dry spell it is likely to be conspicuous by its absence.

Near the top of Flinter Gill you emerge from wooded confines, and to the right Middleton Fell appears. Now enclosed by walls but pleasanter underfoot, the way rises to join the Occupation Road. Here a beautifully composed scene awaits as lower Dentdale leads the eye to the grouping of the Howgill Fells. The 'Occy' Road contours around the northern flank of Great Coum, being an old packhorse way and service road for the enclosures. It is the perfect platform for views over the dale, but sections have suffered badly in recent years under the wheels of motor vehicles. Turn right along this wide lane for a long stride following it until you join the Dent-Barbon road.

Turn briefly right along the road before a footpath sign points the way through a gate on the left. A sketchy track crosses to a stile in the far corner. From it head left towards the steep slope, and a path materialises to swing right as a superb green promenade. All too soon a gateway is reached before the ruinous Combe House. Here the striking hollow of Combe Scar looms tantalisingly above. This colourful scene – unjustly bereft of rights of way – is chiselled out of the northern flank of Middleton Fell. It is a popular Dentdale landmark, and with its low crags there is more then a hint of Lakeland about it. The path fades at the sad ruin of Combe House: pass round the far side and follow a barely discernible wall-line heading away.

Combe Scar from Barth Bridge.

Down the field a farm track is joined to head left down through a gateway. Through the next gateway, forsake the track and make a bee-line for the farm buildings of Tofts. A slab footbridge over a tree-lined beck precedes a clamber up the opposite bank. Pass between the buildings and out along the drive, dropping gradually down to a back road at Underwood. Gawthrop is just minutes along to the right, a picturesque grouping of cottages and farms well off the beaten track.

Gawthrop is vacated by a short-lived farm drive on the left, just 30 m after the last track off to the right (after the phone box). Cross the edge of a farmyard to a gate to the right, and descend the field alongside a wooded gill. Part-way down, the path spends a few metres in its confines. It then resumes down the field side, fading by the bottom corner. Continue down to a stile level with an island barn, resuming on the other side to descend to a stile onto the road.

Church Bridge, Dent.

Go left to reach Barth Bridge, and without crossing it take a stile on the right. A path heads directly across two small fields to gain the riverbank, then shadows the Dee upstream until briefly ushered onto the road. A path soon dives back into the fields, clinging tightly to the river to arrive at Church Bridge. Dent has been visible up to the right during this section, and all that remains is to turn up the road to re-enter the village.

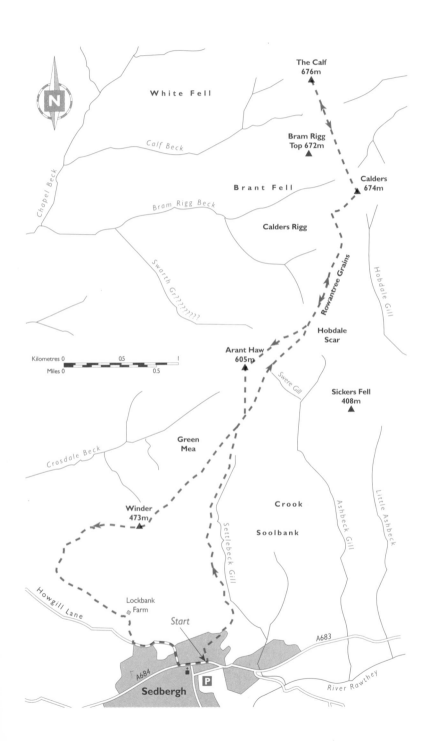

The Calf
676m

White Fell

Bram Rigg
Top 672m

Calf Beck

Calders
674m

Brant Fell

Chapel Beck

Bram Rigg Beck

Calders Rigg

Swarth Gr?????????

Rowantree Grains

Hobdale Gill

Hobdale
Scar

Arant Haw
605m

Kilometres 0   0.5   1
Miles 0   0.5

Swere Gill

Sickers Fell
408m

Green
Mea

Crosdale Beck

Winder
473m

Crook

Soolbank

Settlebeck Gill

Ashbeck Gill

Little Ashbeck

Howgill Lane

Lockbank
Farm

Start

A683

A684

P

Sedbergh

River Rawthey

HIGH ON THE HOWGILL FELLS

S edbergh is the largest community in the Yorkshire Dales National Park, yet its isolation has helped it avoid the excesses of commercialism. Ceded to Cumbria in 1974, Sedbergh was previously in the north western extremity of the West Riding of Yorkshire. This small market town boasts an unparalleled position on the lower slopes of the Howgill Fells, and the outlook on three sides is, in fact, of fells. This is the edge of the Dales, and to the west of the town runs the river Lune. In the neighbourhood of Sedbergh the rivers Dee, Clough and Rawthey join forces to swell the waters of the Lune.

Aside from the imposing Howgill Fells, Sedbergh itself is dominated by its public school. Founded in the early 16th century this famous establishment boasts some celebrated old boys, including a popular sporting hero, none other than Will Carling, who went on to become the most successful recent captain of England's rugby union team. Two centuries earlier it helped educate a Dent man, from five miles up the road, who went on to become Professor of Geology at Cambridge (see also Walk 12).

Most other features of interest will be found on or near the lengthy main street, including St. Andrew's church. In its attractive wooded surround, it dates back in part to the 12th century: its dedication is a common one in these parts, due to Scottish influence. There is also a National Park Centre, with a wide range of information and publications available.

Leave the main street by Joss Lane rising past the main car park. It swings up to the right as 'to the fell' signs ease the way out of town. From its demise at a gate a farm road to Hill takes over, while your way slants left to the top corner of the field. A path climbs with Settlebeck Gill to gain the open fell at a quaint kissing gate: through it, seats offer an early rest.

INFORMATION

Distance: 13 km (8 miles).

Start and finish: Sedbergh. There are two car parks in the town.

Terrain: A fellwalk over extremely accommodating terrain. The experienced will readily take to this in trainers on a settled day, but as with any other fellwalk, caution is required. In the colder seasons any kind of conditions can be faced on the tops, and walkers should be adequately prepared and equipped with suitable food and drink.

Public transport: Sedbergh is served by infrequent bus from Kendal.

Refreshments: Cafes and pubs in Sedbergh, nothing en route.

Opening hours: *National Park Centre, Main Street:* open daily Easter-Oct 1000–1600.

Take the green path slanting up behind, quickly doubling back to run high above Settlebeck Gill. Slowly deflected away by a tiny sidestream, the path reaches an upland basin. Take the path bearing right, back to the ravine, and continue upstream. Some time later, with the beck's confines tamer, a fork is reached. Continue with the gill to rise to a broad path on the slopes of Arant Haw. This is a great moment, with the next stage climbing to Arant Haw and beyond clear ahead of you, and the Lune Valley and Lakeland skyline appearing to the west.

You now have the main path of the Howgill Fells underfoot. This popular walkers' thoroughfare links Sedbergh with the Calf, and its green carpet transports you across Arant Haw's upper slopes to a distinct brow. The path now sets about the higher reaches of the Howgills, but first falls to a depression before climbing steeply by a fence to the cairn on Calders. This subsidiary top is a fine vantage point, resting on the edge of a more pronounced drop than the principal summit.

The Calf now waits ahead, and a grand high level amble ensues. The clear path encounters two minor descents on the way, for the intervening summit of Bram Rigg Top must be crossed (the highest point is

further to the left, though it hardly merits a diversion). The final pull is a very short one to the Ordnance Survey column marking the summit of the Calf, at 676 m the highest point on the Howgills. Its

North-west from the Calf.

panorama features the Cross Fell group to the north and the widely spread hills of the Dales to east and south, but on a clear day the serrated Lakeland skyline to the west will claim most attention.

The return route retraces steps over Calders, indeed you could retrace every single step if so desired. Far nicer, however, to visit a couple of rewarding underlings to prolong the joyous descent. Climbing out of the depression after Calders, leave the main path by bearing right on a vague trod rising effortlessly to Arant Haw's summit.

Calders from Arant Haw.

Leave the scrappy cairn for the southern edge of the broad top, where a clear path makes a no-nonsense descent back to the main path. Bearing right at two successive junctions the ascent of the day's third summit, Winder, is rapidly accomplished on an undemanding stroll over grassy knolls. The way has been entirely apparent since departing Arant Haw, and the Ordnance Survey column and cairn appear well in advance.

From this neat top savour the scene around you: Garsdale is particularly appealing as it burrows deep into high fells. You also have an excellent view up the Lune Gorge into the western Howgills. By dropping down a little way, you can savour an intimate bird's-eye view of Sedbergh, backed by Dentdale stretching into the haze: this is entirely fitting, as Winder is popularly regarded as the town's own 'special' fell.

Howgill Ridges between Arant Haw and Calders.

Leave by a path striking west towards the Lune, an outstanding green way that descends with expansive views westwards, including, in the valley below, the old railway through the Lune Gorge, including the Lune Viaduct. Descend to within yards of the intake wall, then turn left to trace a narrow path through bracken, meeting up with the wall as Sedbergh appears ahead. A super way slants down to the rear of Lockbank Farm. Here a gate precedes a short green way down to the farmyard, straight through and out onto its drive. This permissive path leads down onto Howgill Lane. Turn left to finish.

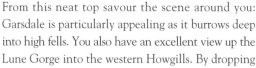

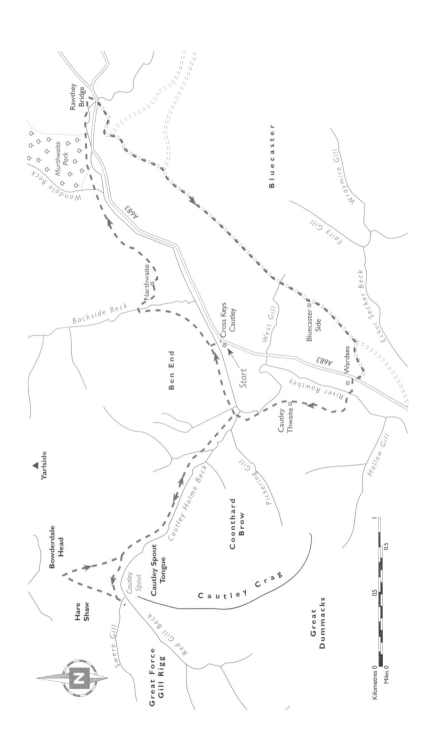

CAUTLEY SPOUT

This is a justifiably famous corner of the Howgills, with more than the obvious charms. The lengthy preamble to Cautley Spout can be omitted by turning left after the opening footbridge, and following the main path around to the falls: this reduces the walk to something in the order of 5 km (3 miles).

The Cross Keys is that rare creature, the temperance inn. Though labelled Cautley there is no definable centre, just a scattering of farms, dwellings and a church along the Sedbergh road.

Cross the footbridge over the Rawthey just above the inn, and go straight ahead onto a wide track. Turn right along it, continuing as a pleasant green path to ford Backside Beck (a challenge after a wet spell) before a short pull to Narthwaite. Leave the farm buildings by the drive on the right, following it almost all the way down to the main road. A gate on a sharp bend, however, points the way along a lesser track which ends at a wood. Through a gate, ford a stream to follow a path along the wood bottom, and when the fence turns right it slants down to follow the Rawthey upstream.

The river Rawthey flows for 26 km from near the lonely summit of Baugh Fell to its acceptance into the Lune beyond Sedbergh. On the journey there it absorbs the waters of the Clough and the Dee. All is preciously unspoilt hereabouts, and in the neighbourhood of this walk the river exudes all its charms, flowing along a green valley bottom flanked by bare fells.

INFORMATION

Distance: 10 km (6 miles).

Start and finish: Cross Keys Inn, Cautley, on the A683 Sedbergh-Kirkby Stephen road. Layby adjacent.

Terrain: Very mixed: good paths but can be wet and rough underfoot. Boots advisable.

Public transport: None.

Refreshments: Temperance inn at the start, nothing en route.

Cautley Spout.

Emerging from the trees to cross a brace of fields, a tiny stream is crossed (by a bridge, at last!) to rise onto the road just above Rawthey Bridge. Rawthey Bridge marks the old Yorkshire-Westmorland boundary and, as a result, the illogical National Park boundary also. Between the prosaically titled Backside Beck and the bridge you therefore tread a mile of old Westmorland.

Within a few yards of crossing the bridge take a gate on the left, from where a track heading away almost at once turns sketchily right in distinctly 'moist' environs. Soon the track improves, and after a gentle rise it starts to run parallel with, but high above the main road. On this section from Rawthey Bridge to beyond Bluecaster you tread the old road to Kirkby Stephen, once the main highway through these hills. Constructed well above the valley floor, it now forms a green promenade with truly outstanding views across to the eastern Howgills: semi-wild ponies graze this open fell. Shortly after going past Bluecaster Cottage a gate is reached at a lane head, and just after it take a gate on the right to descend a sunken track onto the road.

Cross the main road and go down a farm road past Wardses. The farm bridge over the Rawthey here is surprisingly high: note the intense clarity of the water. The track continues through the fields to Cautley

Cautley Crag from the
Cross Keys.

Above Cautley Crag.

Thwaite Farm. Keep straight on through two gates and to the right of a barn, then go a little left to a gate to emerge on a good path. Soon Cautley Holme Beck is crossed by a basic bridge, from where a path runs along to the foot of Cautley Spout. To enjoy a closer look, cross the side beck and tackle the steep path by the gill. Caution is urged when peering into the lower fall, which is partially obscured by hardy foliage.

Cautley Crag and Spout combine to form the grandest scene in the Howgill Fells. The steep crag extends for the best part of a mile to an abrupt end at the Spout. Cautley Spout is a series of waterfalls which tumble in rapid succession for several hundred metres to the valley floor.

Continuing up, the upper falls are free of obstruction and can be savoured in a more leisurely fashion. At the top the path levels out, and here leave it after locating a trod along to the right. After a steady traverse it fades, leaving you to slant down to the incisive pass of Bowderdale Head. Turning right a good path forms, to return with the side beck to the foot of the Spout. Omitting Cautley Holme Beck, head back round the base of Yarlside on the 'tourist' path, turning upstream with the Rawthey to soon return to the footbridge at the start.

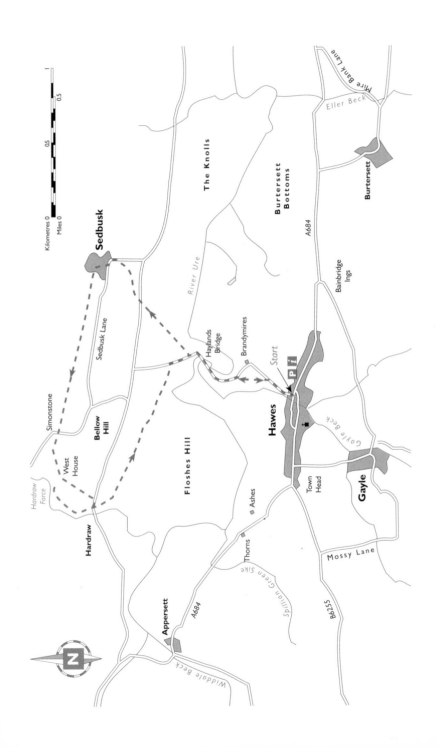

HARDRAW FORCE – THE BIG DROP

This is a superbly varied little walk, with extensive views across Wensleydale and a magnificent waterfall as the focal point.

Hawes is the 'capital' of Upper Wensleydale, a lively, colourful market town to which all visitors are drawn. The place gains even greater character at its Tuesday market, when there are, happily, as many locals in evidence as there are tourists. Hawes has retained an unconventional layout, including some cobbled road, and a leisurely exploration really is essential. Once the last stop on the Wensleydale branch line, its station has been put to use as a National Park Centre, with a wide range of information and publications available. Also keeping the station yard alive is the Dales Countryside Museum, where you can learn of local life and industries of the past

Two surviving local industries now have the added benefit of being tourist attractions. Only yards away is the fascinating ropemakers, where you can witness the ropemaker's art and buy a finished product all under one roof: you name it and they'll put the 'twist' in it, from dog's leads to washing lines! Also in the town is the Wensleydale Creamery, a local success story built on potential disaster when closure loomed in the early 1990s. The story of cheese complements the chance to view traditional cheese-making. Other places of interest include the parish church of St. Margaret; a modern youth hostel on this major staging post on the Pennine Way; and a celebrated antiquarian bookshop.

From the car park take the path by the old railway bridge up onto the road, and turn right to follow it out of town. Within a few yards a track heads off to the left, and with it a gate signals the route of the Pennine Way, whose flagged course is followed to rejoin the road a little further on. Cross Haylands Bridge over the Ure, then take a stile which soon appears on the right,

INFORMATION

Distance: 5 km (3 miles).

Start and finish: Hawes. There is a large National Park car park in the old station yard.

Terrain: Low level walking on field paths, but some parts can be wet underfoot. Trainers are adequate in dry spells.

Public transport: Hawes is served by bus from Leyburn and Richmond, and by infrequent seasonal services, including from Garsdale station on the Settle-Carlisle Railway.

Refreshments: Cafes and pubs in Hawes and Hardraw, hotel at Simonstone.

Opening hours: *Dales Countryside Museum:* open daily Apr-Oct 1000–1700, some winter weekends; small admission charge. *National Park centre:* open daily Easter-Oct 1000–1600, and some winter weekends. *Ropemakers:* open all year Mon-Fri 0900–1730, some summer Sats 1000–1730, free. *Wensleydale Creamery:* open all year Mon-Sat 0930–1700, Sun 1000–1630, admission fee.

a sketchy path going across the field to a small, arched bridge.

From it the path climbs half-right to a stile, from where a large field is crossed to a stile in the top corner. Cross straight over the road to a stile opposite,

Hawes and Dodd Fell from Sedbusk.

and of the two paths leaving it, take the fainter one bearing across to the right. Beyond a stile it rises up past a prominent tree at a wall corner, and across to a stile onto Sedbusk Lane. Rise left into Sedbusk, and turn right at the narrow entrance into the hamlet. This unspoilt collection of farms and cottages looks across the dale to Hawes and beyond from an altitude little under 300 m.

Leave the tiny green by a stile on the left, passing between houses and out into a field. Here commences a long kilometre through a remarkable series of gap-stiles punctuating a string of small fields. Initially they come so thick and fast that the next couple of stiles are usually already in view. The way is obvious throughout, and this gentle stroll allows time to enjoy extensive panoramas over Wensleydale. Rising above Hawes are the unassuming mountains of Wether Fell, Dodd Fell and Widdale Fell. The road to Wharfedale over Fleet Moss (590 m) is clearly in sight.

The chain is broken as a couple of ladder-stiles by a barn complex complete the process. The farm track leads out to the road, with a gap-stile available a little left of the gate. Here the Buttertubs road is joined at the tiny settlement of Simonstone. Go left a few yards then right along the drive to Simonstone Hall, now a hotel. Turn off left at a stile just short of the house, along a field-top and on again to West House Farm. From a stile to its right a path descends two more fields to emerge via a yard into Hardraw. This unassuming hamlet has been made famous by its waterfall, which at around 30 m is claimed to be the highest single drop above ground in England.

Access to Hardraw Force is through the Green Dragon inn, where a charge is made to view the 'private' spectacle: it is but a five minute walk into the increasingly impressive amphitheatre. More so than most, the tiny beck needs to have seen recent rain for the scene to be fully appreciated. The cliff over which the water spills is Hardraw Scaur, or Scar. In the gorge below the force century-old brass band contests have made a revival, and an annual event takes place in early September.

On returning to the inn, cross the road and take a track just left of the bridge. Behind the buildings go left to a small gate from where a good, largely flagged path crosses a series of fields to eventually join a road. Turn right to pick up the outward route, over Haylands Bridge and back into Hawes.

Hardraw Force.

Green Dragon, Hardraw.

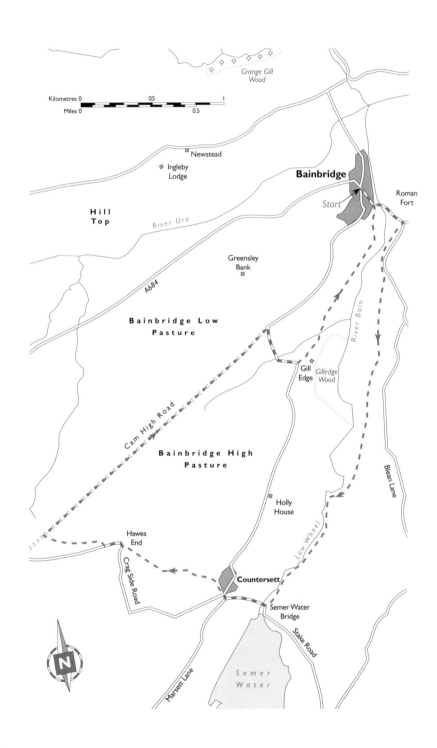

Grange Gill
Wood

Kilometres 0   0.5   1
Miles 0   0.5

Newstead

Ingleby
Lodge

Bainbridge

Roman
Fort

Start

**Hill
Top**

River Ure

Greensley
Bank

A684

**Bainbridge Low
Pasture**

River Bain

Gill
Edge

*Gilledge
Wood*

**Bainbridge High
Pasture**

Cam High Road

Blean Lane

Holly
House

Low Wheel

Hawes
End

Countersett

Crag Side Road

Semer Water
Bridge

Scake Road

N

Marsett Lane

*Semer
Water*

ROMAN STEPS FROM SEMERWATER

This walk is a steady ramble by the shortest river, to a surprisingly extensive lake and along an ancient highway in the heart of Wensleydale.

Bainbridge is an unspoilt village whose houses stand well back from an enormous green. Such is its extent that the effect of the main road cutting across it seems insignificant. Principle features are the stocks which still grace the green, and the whitewashed Rose & Crown, dating back several centuries and possibly the oldest in the dale. The structure which gives the village its name is a shapely platform from which to survey the finest stretch of the river before it sneaks quietly round the backs of the houses.

Historical connections abound. Brough Hill, peering over the houses at the east end of the village, is the site of the Roman fort Braccium. Centuries later the hunting-mad Norman lords based their foresters here in the Forest of Wensleydale. At the inn can be seen a horn which was blown during winter evenings to guide benighted travellers to safety. Its origins go back earlier still, as a warning sound in the days of the forest. Happily, this ancient event survives purely as a quaint custom.

Leave Bainbridge by the main road to Aysgarth at the corner of the green, crossing the bridge over the River Bain and climbing the steep hill. Take a stile on the right just before a junction and head across the pasture, keeping well above the steep drop to the river. Pass to the left of an 'island' field and at the brow of the hill a sketchy path leads on to a stile. Marker posts show the way down the slope beyond, with Semerwater fully in view.

Head on through stiles in intervening walls, and at a ladder-stile bear right to finally join the riverbank. Meeting the Ure at Bainbridge, the River Bain is

INFORMATION

Distance: 10 km (6 miles).

Start and finish: Bainbridge. There is ample parking alongside the spacious green.

Terrain: Field paths and old tracks. Boots advisable.

Public transport: Bainbridge is served by Hawes-Leyburn buses.

Refreshments: Cafe and pub at the start; often an ice cream van midway, in summer.

Bain below Semerwater.

claimed to be the shortest in the county. Your route explores it comprehensively, from its tumbles over rock ledges above Bainbridge to its tranquil meander from Semerwater. It now offers a simple walk upstream to join the road at Semerwater Bridge. Before crossing, have a potter along the lakeshore: its foot is directly in front.

Semerwater was the largest lake in the old North Riding of Yorkshire, an area not lavishly endowed with sheets of water. Not surprisingly it is a popular venue for a variety of watersports, and as a result an association exists to control these activities and help protect birdlife. Prominent on the shore is the mighty Carlow Stone, said to have been dropped here by a giant. Local legend also relates how a visitor, inhospitably treated, caused a whole 'city' to be submerged. What is more certain is that Iron Age lake-dwellings existed here.

Semerwater, looking to Addlebrough.

Resume the walk by crossing the bridge and climbing the steep road to a crossroads at Countersett. This small hamlet boasts an early Friends Meeting House and a mellow old hall, also with strong Quaker connections. Turn right for the hamlet, but just before the first house opt instead for an enclosed track to cottages on the left. Taking a gate by the first dwelling on the left, begin a steep climb to first one and then a second barn. These steep slopes command a superb panorama of Semerwater's side valley. Most prominent feature is the upthrust of Addleborough across the lake. Though a modest 480 m high, it is one of Wensleydale's major landmarks, and is thought to have been the site of a Brigantes' hillfort.

From the barn rise half-left to a stile and continue diagonally up to the wall rising to the far corner. At this point the Semerwater scene is finally left behind. From the stile, follow the wall up to a gate onto the Countersett-Burtersett road at its highest point. Go right for a couple of minutes to reach a stile on the right. A sketchy path passes through a collapsed wall and then fades in rough pasture as it slants down to a stile onto the Cam High Road.

Cam High Road is the Roman road running from Ribblehead to the fort at Bainbridge. The whole of that section forms an exhilarating high level march that can still be enjoyed today in its entirety. Though 'improved' further westward, several miles remain to provide a gem of a traffic-free route. This present walk tramps the easternmost section which points itself unerringly at Bainbridge. The views embrace an unrivalled length of Wensleydale, including Hawes, Askrigg, numerous individual features and most of the surrounding fells.

Turn right to follow the arrow-like course of the road until eventual hi-jacked by a modern road. Head up this as far as Gill Edge, just ahead, and turn left along its drive. From a stile on the left descend to another at the field bottom, from where a sketchy path crosses two fields to a barn. A clearer path runs on to two further stiles, and from a gate above the river descends the wall side to the edge of Bainbridge. The path becomes enclosed to run past cottages before re-emerging onto the village green.

The Green, Bainbridge.

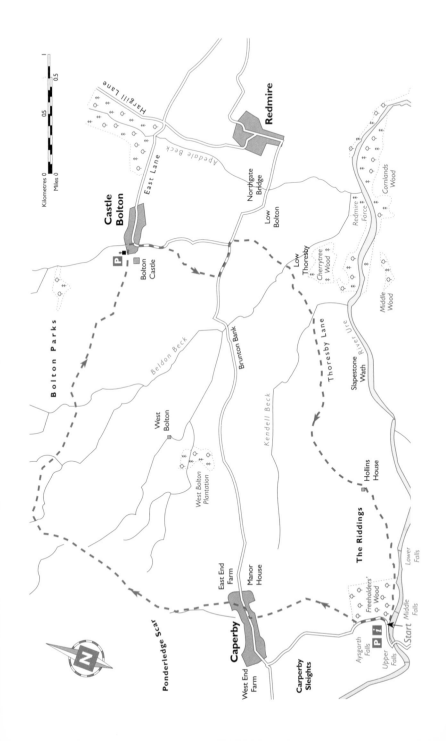

Miles 0
Kilometres 0   0.5   0.5   1

Hargill Lane

Redmire

East Lane

Apedale Beck

Castle
Bolton

Northgate
Bridge

Bolton Castle

Low Bolton

Bolton Parks

Low
Thoresby

Cherrytree
Wood

Redmire Force

Cornlands
Wood

Middle
Wood

Beldon Beck

Brunton Bank

Thoresby Lane

Slapestone
Wath

River Ure

Kendell Beck

West
Bolton

West Bolton
Plantation

Hollins
House

The Riddings

Lower
Falls

Ponderledge Scar

East End
Farm

Manor
House

Freeholders'
Wood

Middle
Falls

Caperby

West End
Farm

Aysgarth
Falls

Upper
Falls

Carperby
Sleights

Start

N

CASTLE BOLTON

Two of Wensleydale's most famous features are visited on this easy ramble, one natural, one the work of man.

First port of call before leaving the car park should be the National Park Centre, with a wide range of information and publications available. A more down to earth port of call is the toilet block, opened in 1995 and featuring a 'compost' system that uses no water: notices warn against young children falling in!

From the car park return to the road and turn left under the old railway bridge. Just after the station yard take a gate on the right to enter a wood. A path rises through trees, crossing a wide, green path to a hidden stile ahead, from where a string of gap-stiles point the way half-right through the fields. At the last stile, turn left to a stile onto the farm road of Low Lane.

Cross straight over to pass through a long, narrow field, and from a stile on the right near the end, continue on to a gate between houses to emerge onto the road in Carperby, opposite the Wheatsheaf Inn. It was here that the real life 'James Herriot', TV vet, spent his honeymoon. Carperby is one of the dale's most attractive villages, with virtually all its sturdy stone dwellings lining the road. Standing well back from the valley bottom, it was once of greater importance as testified by the market cross on the narrow green.

Turn right a short distance and head up the first lane on the left. This 'no through road' rises out of the

INFORMATION

Distance: 11 km (7 miles).

Start and finish: Aysgarth. Large National Park car park at Aysgarth Falls, east of the village.

Terrain: Riverside and good field paths, but can be wet and rough underfoot. Boots advisable.

Public transport: Aysgarth is served by Leyburn-Hawes buses.

Refreshments: Cafe at the start; refreshments at Bolton Castle.

Opening hours: *Bolton Castle:* open Mar-Nov daily 1000-1700, possible winter opening; tearoom and gift shop; admission charge. *National Park Centre,* Castle Bolton: open daily Easter-Oct 1000-1600, and some winter weekends.

Aysgarth Churchyard.

village to become a broad track between walls. Beyond a barn keep right at a fork to climb by the wall and round to a gate. A large tract of colourful, rough pasture is entered, and with Bolton Castle in view down-dale, your near level approach to it can be well surveyed. A generally clear green track heads on through bracken to a gate at the far end, then crosses Beldon Beck and runs a little less clearly to a gate in the right-hand wall.

Bolton Castle.

From here the track becomes wide and clear through half a dozen more fields towards the imposing bulk of Bolton Castle. Through a narrow wood the track leads to the very walls of the castle.

From a distance the majestic pile of Bolton Castle belies its ruinous condition. Originally a 14th century manor house, it was converted into a castle by Richard, Lord Scrope. Mary, Queen of Scots was a famous guest, being imprisoned here from 1568 to 1569. The labyrinth of an interior is well worth exploring, with tearoom and gift shop as modern day additions. To correct a commonly made error, the village is Castle Bolton and the castle is Bolton Castle.

Between castle and church you emerge onto the village street alongside the spacious green separating two intermittent rows of cottages. Comprehensively overshadowed by its castle, the village of Castle Bolton is appealing in its own right. Standing almost at the castle wall, St Oswald's church dates back more than 600 years and reveals a surprisingly spacious interior. From the corner here descend this road to leave the village. Soon a track forks right between barns, descending to two houses and the defunct railway line. Across the old line a leafy snicket drops down to join a road.

Go left along the road as far as the Castle Bolton junction, then take a stile on the right. Cross to the far end of the field, and from the stile bear right down to another stile in the very bottom left corner. It leads to a small footbridge onto Thoresby Lane. Turning right, the lane soon ends at Low Thoresby Farm, but at a gate to the right it returns as a delectable green byway. Little altered for centuries, its snaking route between hedgerows is a joy throughout. It finally terminates just beyond a junction with aptly named Watery Lane, which goes down to ford the Ure. From a stile into a field follow the wall away to the next, then bear left over the brow to a stile near the far corner.

A farm track is joined leading down to Hollin House, keeping right at the first building to a gateway before the barn complex. Take a gap-stile on the left to slant down to a gate from where a green track heads away. As it swings down the large field head straight across to a stile. Part way along the fence side, drop down left to another stile.

At this point you meet up with the terminus of the ever popular Aysgarth Falls path, and just below are the Lower Falls. A distinct gap in the cliffs permits a cul-de-sac descent to the water's-edge vantage point. A well trodden path then heads up river, passing by a short, circular detour to a more intimate viewpoint for the Lower Falls. Up above, the path temporarily vacates the woodland before entering Freeholder's Wood to rapidly reach the Middle Falls viewing platform. Only a little further, you emerge onto the road just below the car park entrance.

Middle Falls, Aysgarth.

To include the Upper Falls turn down the road to the best viewpoint, Yore Bridge, from where a path leads back to the car park.

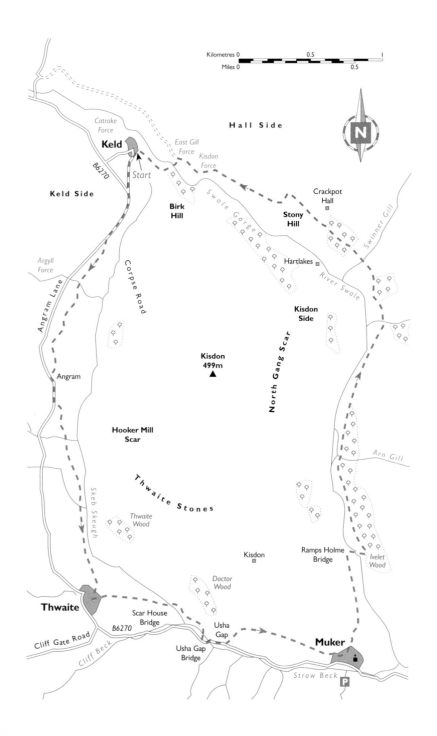

Kilometres 0   0.5   1
Miles 0   0.5

N

Catrake
Force

Keld

*East Gill
Force*

*Kisdon
Force*

H a l l   S i d e

B6270

Start

Keld Side

**Birk
Hill**

Swale Gorge

**Stony
Hill**

Crackpot
Hall

Swinner Gill

*Argyll
Force*

Hartlakes

River Swale

Angram Lane

Corpse Road

**Kisdon
Side**

**Kisdon
499m** ▲

N o r t h   G a n g   S c a r

Angram

**Hooker Mill
Scar**

Arn Gill

Skeb Skeugh

T h w a i t e   S t o n e s

*Thwaite
Wood*

Kisdon

Ramps Holme
Bridge

*Ivelet
Wood*

*Doctor
Wood*

Thwaite

Scar House
Bridge

Cliff Gate Road

B6270

Cliff Beck

Usha Gap
Bridge

Usha
Gap

Muker

Straw Beck

P

THROUGH THE SWALE GORGE

This is one of the most beautiful walks in the Dales, with stunning scenery in the peerless surroundings of Upper Swaledale.

Keld is the first outpost of any size in Swaledale, for above here are only isolated dwellings beneath the moors. The heart of this Norse settlement is a tiny square below the main road and high above the Swale. Keld is best known for its waterfalls, Catrake Force being just round the back of the square, East Gill Force on this walk, and Kisdon Force just off-route. Keld also marks the junction of Pennine Way and Wainwright's Coast to Coast Walk.

Leave the square by the lane up to the main road, and turn left along it for a couple of minutes to where a rough track drops down to the left. Not your route, on this occasion, this is the first section of a 'corpse road'. Its purpose is aptly described in its title: this was the route by which coffin parties would carry the deceased of the upper dale down to the church at Grinton, which until the 1580 offered the only consecrated ground in the entire valley. Just past it a stile will be found. Here begins a faint, at times invisible path through flower-rich meadows, rendered easy to follow by regular punctuation by stiles. A good dozen are encountered, most being visible well in advance. A further guide is the fact that all the isolated field barns are passed on their right side.

The road is rejoined after skirting the hamlet of Angram, and within a couple of minutes is vacated again at a stile on the left. Once more the stiles make life easy as you slope down to join a tiny beck. Thwaite is approached on a path composed of flags

INFORMATION

Distance: 10 km (6 miles).

Start and finish: Keld. There is a small amount of parking in the square, just down from the main road, and a farm there sometimes opens up its yard for parking. Otherwise, park on the main road above the village.

Terrain: Very easy walking on field paths and tracks. Trainers are adequate in summer.

Public transport: Keld is served by bus from Richmond on Tuesdays and Saturdays.

Refreshments: Teas, ices in Keld (seasonal), cafe in Thwaite, pub in Muker.

Angram, Upper Swaledale.

overgrown with time. It is entered at the point where the Pennine Way departs: after a look round and possibly a cuppa, return to this point. Thwaite was birthplace, in the latter half of the 19th century, of Richard and Cherry Kearton, brothers who went on to become pioneers in the early days of nature photography. They were the first to fully illustrate nature books with photographs, while the younger Cherry later achieved acclaim with his wildlife films. Not for them the pocket camera, but an unwieldy collection of equipment that when carried round the dale left little room for flask, sandwiches and other such luxuries! A long established guest house recalls their name; highly regarded by ramblers, it doubles as a place of refreshment in amongst the cottages and farms that make up the remainder of Thwaite.

Leave along the short lane in front of the cafe, and at the end a Pennine Way sign points the way through a short ginnel and a couple of stiles into a field. Here the Way strikes left, but you continue roughly parallel with a beck on a sketchy path across four fields, to reach a tiny bridge over a beck coming in from the left. Cross the field-bottom beyond and head past a

Muker.

barn to a stile from where a short, enclosed track joins the road at Usha Gap. Go left to the farm and up its drive to a stile on the right. Cross to a stile near the far corner of the field, from where a string of stiles lead across the field-bottoms to enter Muker just behind the pub. The latter stages are again flagged.

With accommodation, shops, cafe and the Farmers Arms, Muker is a good centre for the upper dale, and probably its most picturesque village. Prominent in most views is St Mary's church, first built in 1580 to relieve Grinton's workload by taking the upper dale off its hands. Other interesting buildings are the Literary Institute of 1868 and the school, with tablets proclaiming that the Kearton brothers were pupils here.

Leave Muker by a well-signposted stile beside a gate between buildings at the top of a short lane leading up to and behind the Post office. A well defined path crosses seven fields linked by solid stiles to arrive at the riverbank. Turn right to another stile to follow the Swale downstream a few metres to Ramps Holme Bridge. This, the only crossing of the Swale between Keld and Ivelet Bridge, is an excellent viewpoint for the Swale Gorge upstream. On the opposite bank, drop down left to the river, soon to join a wide track which is accompanied almost all the way back to Keld. On crossing the first inflowing beck, a stroll a short distance up its course earns a fine view of the charming waterfall of Arngill Force.

Continuing by the river, the track crosses a bridge below the ravine of Swinner Gill, once a thriving lead mining site. The track then rises steeply before easing out above an increasingly impressive wooded gorge. A

Near Angram.

track from the ruin of Crackpot Hall is joined, and this same track eventually descends to a farm bridge over East Gill. The amusing name of Crackpot, incidentally, derives from the Norse for 'hole of the crows'. Crackpot Hall was abandoned many decades ago as a result of subsidence caused by lead mining.

At East Gill note the shared 'Pennine Way' and 'Coast to Coast' signpost, while immediately beneath is the entirely delightful East Gill Force. Drop down the far side of the waterfall to view it, and then, just below is a footbridge over the Swale. From it take the path climbing right to a gate, and within minutes Keld is re-entered.

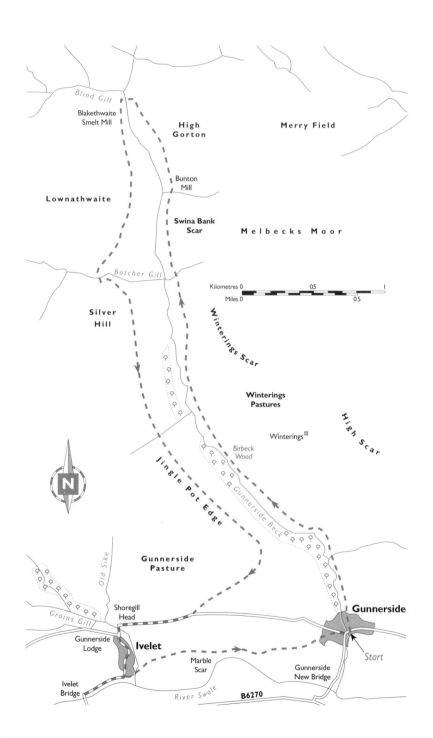

LEAD MINING IN GUNNERSIDE GILL

INFORMATION

Distance: 12 km (7 miles).

Start and finish: Gunnerside. Small parking area by the bridge in the village centre.

Terrain: Rough but easy, steep ground in the gill followed by meadow paths. Boots recommended.

Public transport: Gunnerside is served by bus from Richmond.

Refreshments: Cafe and pub in Gunnerside, nothing en route.

This walk takes you on a fascinating exploration of a deeply confined valley. Extensive lead mining remains stir the imagination, while lush meadows add a soothing conclusion. Overall, it is an absolute feast of colour.

Gunnerside, like its neighbours, had its heyday in lead mining times, when it was a busy centre for the once thriving industry. Again in common with neighbouring villages, it is now a sleepy place. It was founded by the Norsemen, and it would appear that the Gunnar of the name was a Viking chieftain: until recently the Kings Head sported a superb pictorial sign depicting the said invader.

Although lead was mined in these parts at least as long ago as Roman times, the 19th century was far and away its heyday. For a time, Swaledale produced around half of the total of Yorkshire Dales lead. More men had mining-related work than in farming, though this was no 'Klondyke' boom time. Hours were long and the dangers all too apparent. A long walk to work was followed by hours underground in appalling conditions. Winning the ore from the dark holes by simple candlelight was a labour-intensive and dangerous job, though more fell victim to prolonged exposure to fumes and damp than to accidents.

Mines took the form of levels or shafts: levels ran directly into the hillside, while vertical shafts sank deep down. Progressing from picks and shovels, gunpowder was increasingly used to blast the rock, with the ore brought out on carts on small tramways. The onset of the Industrial Revolution brought more mechanised methods, but it certainly would never have become comfortable in the gloomy depths. New small-scale operations often began by the process of 'hushing'. A hush was created by the release of previously dammed-up water, which tore away the hillside and, if you were lucky, revealed a worthwhile amount of lead ore.

Ore was transported from the often exposed mines by ponies and tramways to be sorted. At the crushing mills, usually further down a side valley, the rock was broken down to discard the unwanted stone from the lead ore. This was yet another process in which water played a part, with waterwheels providing power before more mechanised methods arrived.

At the smelt mill the lead ore was placed in a furnace, often fired by peat, wood or coal, from where it was run off to form blocks, or 'pigs', of lead. The notoriously toxic fumes produced by the smelting process were carried away from the mill by long flues built just below ground, to escape into the air by way of tall chimneys.

Late in the 19th century the slump began, and it was a rapid decline. The main cause was the spread of cheap foreign imports: Swaledale's population plunged from 7000 to 2000. Many sought work in the coal mines of Durham or Lancashire's cotton mills, or even crossed the Atlantic in their search for a new life.

In Gunnerside Gill.

The village stands astride its own beck, which apart from a level half kilometre from here to the Swale, spends all of its time tumbling down the deep gill immediately above the village. Gunnerside Gill, even without its open air lead mining 'museum', is arguably the most impressive in the Dales. For a good 6 km its steep sides sweep uninterruptedly down to the beck, exhibiting scale and colour of Lakeland proportions.

The lead mines are as much a part of Swaledale as the waterfalls of Keld, and Gunnerside Gill is an excellent venue for their inspection. Two former crushing mills are visited, each with a long row of bunkers for storing the ore. There are also some classic 'hushes' facing each other across the gill. The return path surveys all these features from a splendid, detached platform. A gloomy day should be no deterrent to this walk: if anything, lingering cloud adds an almost tangible eeriness to the scene, assisted by the spirits of old miners, perhaps?

Leave the bridge in the village centre by a wide track (on the pub side of the bridge) following the beck upstream. After you are deflected round Gunnerside Hall, the beckside is rejoined and a path becomes clear to remain with it for some time. On entering denser trees, a stile admits to a long sliver of woodland from where you rise above the beck. This early part of the walk, through beautiful woodland, contrasts strongly with the bleak scenes which will soon dominate it. The wood is left in impressive surrounds as you near Gunnerside Beck again, now running on through several stiles to arrive at the site of a crushing mill.

Keep left of the ruins along the flat pasture, and a path rises to further stiles. A wide, green path slants up the fellside above that last stile, soon levelling out to run parallel with the beck, now far below. An amazing scene of devastation greets the eye as the extensive lead workings at Bunton are approached. Just beyond the last ruin in the immediate workings the path arrives at a crossroads: the left branch works its way down to the beck and then follows it up the gill floor to Blakethwaite smelt mill.

At the terminus of the walk, Blakethwaite smelt mill served the mines higher up. It was built around 1820 and offers much of interest to the inquisitive. Its best surviving feature is the peat store, whose ruinous form might be equally at home at Fountains Abbey. Amidst the ruins a large slab takes you over the beck, and any exploration might include a couple of hundred metres'

Blakethwaite Smelt Mill.

detour on a path up the west bank of the beck for a closer look at Blakethwaite Force. Enthusiasts can continue still further up the gill to reach the Blakethwaite lead mines and dams before returning to the smelt mill.

Back at the smelt mill, the return leg of the walk begins by crossing the inflowing Blind Gill, from where a superb green way rises gently back above the beck. Avoid any deviations and continue to rise to the last mining remains of the day at Lownathwaite Mines, featuring North Hush. The track now becomes level before it contours around Botcher Gill. Here you merge with a wide shooters' track, which beyond a gate commences a very gradual descent along Jingle Pot Edge, high above Gunnerside Gill.

Ivelet Bridge.

The track eventually curves sharply right, slanting down the hillside to join an unfenced road along the base of the fell. Turn right along this, and at a junction by Gunnerside Lodge just ahead, turn down to the left into Ivelet. A detour of no more than ten minutes down the road will provide a look at Ivelet Bridge, the shapeliest structure to cross the Swale.

Back in the hamlet, locate a little drive on the right (in ascent) leading to a tiny footbridge on Shore Gill. The final stage now heads across countless meadows punctuated by a string of stiles. A bend of the Swale adds further interest at Marble Scar. Beyond here the way strikes off for the village, reaching a gate to enter modern housing, passing left of the school and along a lane back into the village centre.

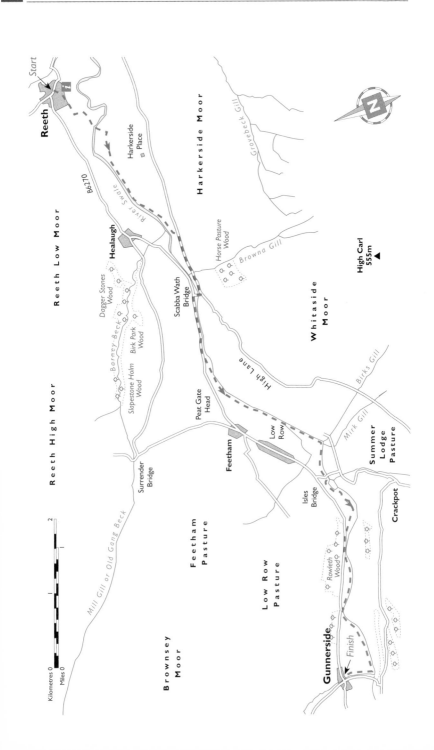

THE ROYAL ROAD THROUGH SWALEDALE

The royal road through Swaledale is not the winding B6270, but the footpaths that trace the banks of this beautiful river. The key to this is the scenic Swaledale bus journey, which, to be fair, does make use of that trusty road. Indeed, on Tuesdays and Saturdays when the service extends to Keld, you might remain with the Swale all the way to Muker or even Keld.

Capital of upper Swaledale, Reeth caters indiscriminately for dalesfolk and visitors alike. It boasts an enviable position on the slopes of Calver Hill, high above the Swale and Arkle Beck. The village centrepiece is a large, sloping green, with the main buildings stood back on all sides. There is a confident air about this one-time market town which radiates chiefly from the hoary inns and the shops alongside the green. Unfortunately, parking limitations result in an untidy scene around the green in summer months: this is amplified when market traders set up stall on Fridays. Inextricably linked with the lead mining days, Reeth was once much more populous. There is an absorbing folk museum here, while annual agricultural shows and festivals add to the cultural attractions.

From the green, pass along the front of the Kings Arms and Black Bull to the contrastingly tiny green at Anvil

INFORMATION

Distance: 10 km (6 miles).

Start: Reeth. Ample car parking alongside the green.

Finish: Gunnerside.

Terrain: Easy walking on riverside paths and tracks. Trainers would suffice in dry weather.

Public transport: Reeth and Gunnerside are linked by bus originating from Richmond.

Refreshments: Cafes and pubs in Reeth; pub in Low Row, just off route, and at Gunnerside.

Opening hours: *Folk Museum:* open Easter-Oct daily 1030-1730; small admission fee.

Fremington Edge from the Green, Reeth.

Square. Just past the Black Bull, incidentally, you pass above the cellar of the former Half Moon Inn, which extends 15 metres out from the front of the building. Across it, to the right, a sign 'to the river' sends a snicket off between walls. It emerges onto a street: turn left to an early T-junction, then right along the narrow lane to its demise at the last house. This continues as a rough lane. At the end turn left down a narrow, leafy footway to emerge just above the river. Bear right through two fields to reach the suspension footbridge over the Swale.

The first section, though regularly walked, is not actually a right of way. The true way heads directly away from the bridge to the foot of the bank, then turns right past a section of wall. When the wall turns away, the bridleway takes the gate on the right and slants back to the riverbank. Simply forge on upstream in glorious surrounds. For much of the way, the meadows alongside have encroached onto the wooded bank. This delectable section ends at a stile opposite Healaugh, where a guidepost sends the path up to join the wall on the left.

Healaugh and Calver Hill.

This rises steadily above the river, but if you are disappointed at leaving it, think again. The ensuing section is arguably finer still, for in addition to the river below, you have truly outstanding views across to

Healaugh backed by Calver Hill, and far up the dale beyond Low Row. The icing on the cake is the lush, grassy way beneath your feet. Simply remain with the wall until just past an intervening fence. Here, at a faint fork, bear left on the grassy way up to a gate, just above which the unfenced moor road to Harkerside is joined.

Continue along the quiet back road as far as an early junction, then turn right over Scabba Wath Bridge and up to the main valley road. Go left for a good kilometre, being wary of traffic, and at the first opportunity take advantage of a footpath signposted to Isles Bridge. The path descends through Feetham Wood to the river and follows it upstream, clinging to its bank the whole way to Isles Bridge. This section, even by Swaledale standards, is sheer pleasure: virtually the entire length is lined with trees.

Swaledale above Healaugh.

Don't cross Isles Bridge but go straight over the road to a stile opposite, sticking with the river only until the first bend. As the river turns away an intermittent path strikes a direct course through the fields, a large pasture preceding two fences before arriving at a stile just before a crumbling barn. From it, join the road as it approaches the returning Swale. As the road rises away, rejoin the river's wooded bank, a path now clinging to it until forced back up onto the road at a steep, wooded bank.

This time the road is left at once, by a gate into a field. Drop steeply to regain the Swale's bank, which is followed pleasurably back to Gunnerside New Bridge. Just before Gunnerside Beck and the bridge, take a gate by a barn for a delightful finish by way of stiles and small enclosures into Gunnerside, emerging rather tidily by the King's Head.

Gunnerside, like its neighbours, had its heyday in lead mining times, when it was a busy centre for the thriving industry. Again in common with neighbouring villages, it is now a sleepy place. It was founded by the Norsemen, and it would appear that Gunnar was a Viking chieftain: until recently the pub sported a superb pictorial sign depicting the said invader.

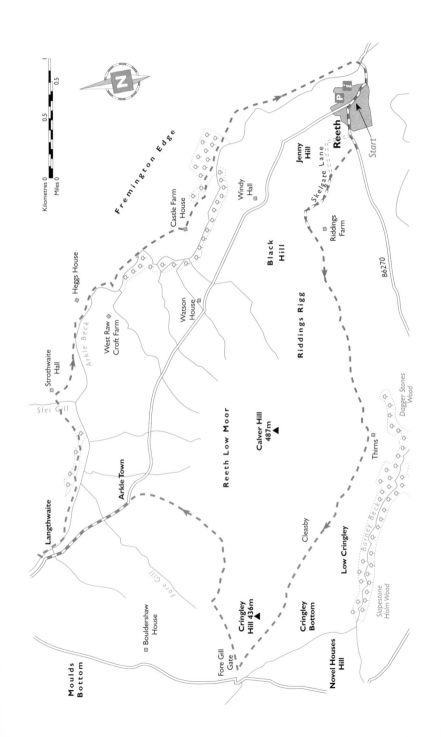

ALL FEATURES GREAT AND SMALL

Calver Hill is Swaledale's shapeliest hill, and Arkengarthdale its major side-valley. Together they form an excellent ramble, combining spacious heather moorland and winding, tree-lined beckside. The televised adventures of Britain's most celebrated vet add a strong underlying theme.

INFORMATION

Distance: 13 km (8 miles).

Start and finish: Reeth. Ample car parking alongside the green.

Terrain: Mixed walking over moorland and by riverside. Boots recommended.

Public transport: Reeth is served by bus from Richmond.

Refreshments: Cafes and pubs in Reeth; pubs in Langthwaite.

Opening hours: *Folk Museum:* open Easter-Oct daily 1030-1730; small admission fee.

Calver Hill.

Focal point of Upper Swaledale, Reeth is prime Herriot country: the film version of Skeldale House looks over the green – can you spot it? Reeth itself is described more fully at the start of Walk 20.

From the top corner of the green, head along the up-dale road as far as the school, and turn up a short-lived snicket on its near side. Emerging into a field, bear left up to a stile part-way up the opposite wall, continuing up to a stile onto a walled snicket. This is Skelgate and is followed up to its emergence onto the moorland slopes of Calver Hill. Bear left on the path, contouring round above the wall. It passes above Riddings Farm and then remains close to the wall. Keep on it past a break in the wall to reach a wall-corner where paths radiate. The main track declines gently past the old cottage of Moorcock to reach the farm at Thirns.

Turn right along the track, soon rising above the wall to the corner of an island enclosure high above the abandoned house at Nova Scotia. The top side of a similar enclosure is passed, just beyond which it runs on to merge with another track. Now head up to the bottom side of yet another walled enclosure (the path heading straight across the slope here is the Coast to Coast Walk), and an improving path heads away from its far corner to pass above a fenced enclosure.

Directly ahead, the track reasserts itself while breasting the slope of Cringley Hill, and remains clear to run undulatingly on to arrive at the roadside at Fore Gill Gate. The watersplash here is a charming little place, given a degree of fame by the opening shots of the TV series.

Just before the gate, however, is a merging of tracks, and it is this other wide way you follow, doubling back over the northern side of Cringley Hill. A branch to

Langthwaite.

the right detours to an old quarry. Your infallible track eventually descends to join the road through Arkengarthdale. Shortly before the road a branch left cuts a small corner. Turn left, becoming enclosed at a cattle-grid and descending through the hamlet of Arkle Town and along to Langthwaite. Just past the Post Office, turn down the narrow road into the little square.

Langthwaite was the centre of Arkengarthdale's lead mining industry. This tiny village comprises two distinct sections. Along the road through the dale are strewn a miscellany of buildings including St

Mary's church. The other half of the village stands just below the road, grouped on the east bank of the beck. This attractive scene is another that will be instantly recognisable to devotees of Mr Herriot's escapades. In amongst these buildings is the cosy Red Lion Inn. Arkengarthdale's other hostelry is the Charles Bathurst (named after a local landowner) on the road beyond the church.

Turn right immediately behind the first house. A broad track accompanies Arkle Beck downstream before striking away from it into a wood. At a fork keep left, rising out of the trees to cross a field to a gate. Here the main track descends to cross Slei Gill (older name Slee Beck) to arrive at Strothwaite Hall.

Arkle Beck, Reeth.

Head straight along the lane to its demise at a farm, then cross two fields to Arkle Beck. This fast flowing stream rises on bleak moorland near the Tan Hill Inn, and takes its name from Arkle Town. Ignoring the footbridge take the gate ahead, after which the path breaks off the bridleway to remain nearer the beck. This it does for some time before being deflected away from a bend in it by way of blobs of paint decorating numerous trees. From here on the way avoids the beck for some while, crossing fields in a generally straight line to arrive at the prominent Castle Farm House.

From it your route heads away in the same direction, amidst as many collapsed walls as intact ones. Dropping to a long abandoned farm the beck is rejoined, but within yards the path forks, and your choice is the track branching left. This soon passes through a gateway out of the trees and alongside a wall on the right. Note the limekiln on the left here. After two further gateways locate a stile on the right, descending past a barn to two slimline stiles in succession. Follow a wall to another stile and continue on through two more fields. The second of these returns you to the road at Reeth Bridge, graceful gateway to the village.

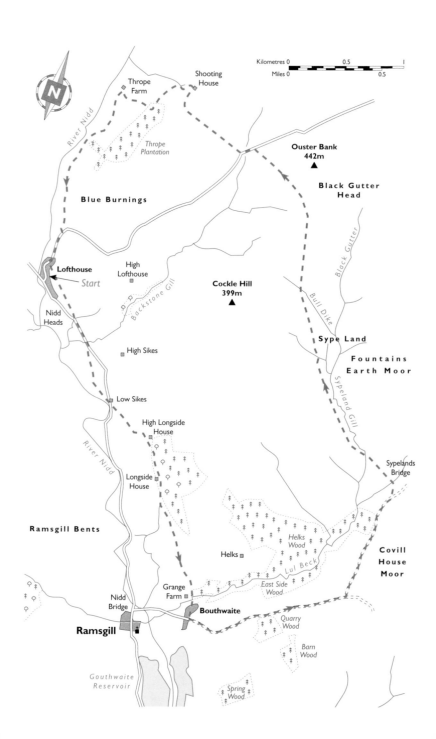

THE NIDDERDALE MOORS

Nidderdale is surrounded by a high moorland skyline, and this excursion links some of the finest heathery tracts with the contrasting delights of the upper valley.

Lofthouse is a tidy village high above the river, its focal point being an attractive corner which includes the homely Post Office. Alongside is a water fountain which bears words worth reading – I'll leave you to work through them! Further down are the village hall, hotel, and the school, which serves all of the upper dale's youngsters. The former station was the highest on the Nidd Valley Light Railway, built to aid construction of the dalehead reservoirs, but exploited to operate a passenger service from Pateley Bridge. It was dismantled after fulfilling its main function.

From the fountain go down the main street a short way, then turn off between the memorial institute and the hotel car park on the left. Just along it, a stile on the right leads to a diagonal field-crossing to another stile. Follow the wall right, crossing a further field before dropping to the road. Have a good look over the wall to locate Nidd Heads – here the true river returns to daylight at a rocky door, after a lengthy underground spell since the environs of Goyden Pot further up-dale.

Turn left for five minutes on the road, then from a stile on the right head half-right to a stile beyond a barn. From a stile by a rusting barn the trackbed of the railway is joined: its grassy embankment leads quickly back onto the road. Cross straight over with the railway, and follow it only as far as a stile, then slant up two fields before the slope eases. Heading away from it, an enclosed path leads below a plantation to Longside House, once a superbly sited youth hostel. Passing between the trees and the rear of the house, the path runs on through a gate to Longside Farm. The views here are truly magnificent, both up and down dale, and across to the moors above Ramsgill.

INFORMATION

Distance: 13 km (8 miles).

Start and finish: Lofthouse. Small car park by the village hall.

Terrain: Largely firm moorland tracks, but varied valley side paths also. Boots advisable.

Public transport: Seasonal Sunday and bank holiday bus from Harrogate via Pateley Bridge.

Refreshments: Pub in Lofthouse, and at Ramsgill, just off-route.

Gouthwaite Reservoir
from above Bouthwaite.

Again keeping round the back, a sketchy path contours across to a stile, then along successive field bottoms. This section enjoys views down the valley to Gouthwaite Reservoir: also clearly discernible is a substantial length of the old railway through the fields below. A stile is reached in front of the wooded environs of Lul Beck. From it drop steeply to a gap-stile, then over a farm bridge into the hamlet of Bouthwaite, Ramsgill's smaller neighbour. Go ahead to a junction of lanes and turn left to a gate, through which a stony track scales the hillside. Suitable halts reveal retrospective views over much of the valley, including Gouthwaite Reservoir again.

When the gradient eases the going underfoot improves, rising to a junction at a wall corner. The track continuing uphill is the old road to Kirkby Malzeard via Dallowgill. These once important highways that linked upper Nidderdale with its monastic landlords today serve only walkers, shooting parties and the occasional off-road biker. Branch left to a second fork, and with a choice of gates, opt for the left fork again.

Across Lul Beck is the heather of Fountains Earth Moor. The moor is named from its early owners, for Fountains Abbey – less than 16 km distant – had an important grange at Bouthwaite. While Nidderdale was in the grip of monastic landlords it was shared by two abbeys that often had their differences: what they did agree on, by and large, was access on certain routes across Fountains' land to enable Byland monks and workers to reach their possessions on the western side of the valley.

The track descends to cross Lul Beck and then a feeder before a steady rise in grand surrounds. For the most part this is a superb green road made and enclosed by walls at the time of the enclosures, in the late 18th and early 19th centuries. In due course it rises to a junction with a firm shooters' track. Go left along this to slant gently down to the road out of Lofthouse.

This moorland road to Masham is the only exit from the valley above Pateley Bridge, and even this was only made fit for motor traffic in the 1960s. Turn left a very short way, then right along a firm track. This quickly reaches a dramatic edge above the upper dale, a stunning moment. Continue north along Thrope Edge to a prominent shooting house. From the road far below this looks like a church silhouetted on the skyline.

Memorial Tap, Lofthouse.

Just after the shooting house, the steep descent begins. A path zigzags down to a gate then heads a little more gently left before swinging sharp right on reaching a wood. From the gate at the bottom follow a fence left to a gate in it. Descend to a barn and onto the track behind Thrope Farm. Thrope had its own watermill until a century ago, and is the site of a small grange of Fountains Abbey. Turn left along this track, Thrope Lane, which leads unerringly along to the moor road just above Lofthouse.

Nidderdale from Thrope Edge.

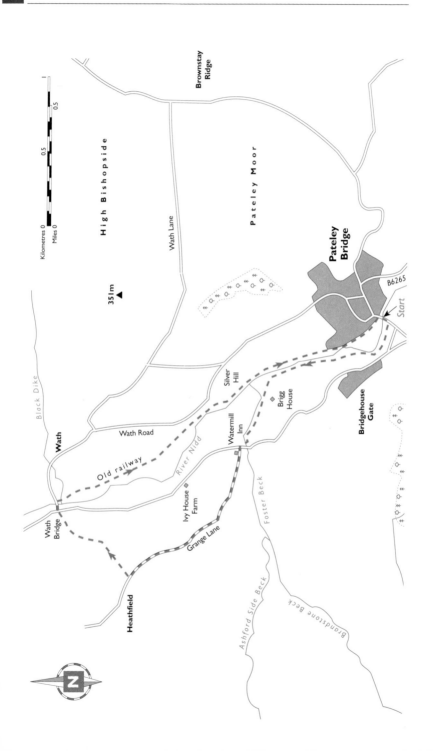

High Bishopside

Brownstay Ridge

Wath Lane

Pateley Moor

Pateley Bridge

B6265

Start

351m

Black Dike

Wath

Silver Hill

Brigg House

Bridgehouse Gate

Wath Road

Watermill Inn

Old railway

River Nidd

Wath Bridge

Ivy House Farm

Foster Beck

Grange Lane

Heathfield

Ashford Side Beck

Brandstone Beck

Kilometres 0   0.5   0.5
Miles 0   0.5   1

THE HEART OF NIDDERDALE

Pateley Bridge is a busy little town, and the undisputed heart of Nidderdale. It draws from far and wide: to Nidderdale folk it is the hub of dale life, to visitors it is the first stop, and the key to the upper dale. The award winning Nidderdale Museum displays over 4,000 items of days past, which includes Pateley's industry too: while much evidence of railways, quarrying and lead mining remains, they are all history. The river Nidd remains as lovely as ever, and paths wait to draw the walker in every direction.

From the foot of the High Street cross the bridge and turn immediately into the park on the right. Remaining on the wooded riverbank, a good path (initially surfaced) leads through a caravan site before

INFORMATION

Distance: 7 km (4 miles).

Start and finish: Pateley Bridge. Car park in the town centre.

Terrain: Varies from riverbank to woodland and moorland. Good paths but boots advisable.

Public transport: Pateley Bridge is served by bus from Harrogate.

Refreshments: Cafes and pubs in Pateley Bridge; pub at Foster Beck and at Wath.

Opening hours: *Nidderdale Museum:* open Easter-Sep daily, 1400–1700, Oct-Easter Sun only, 1400–1700; small admission fee.

High Street, Pateley Bridge.

gaining open fields. In the second field the path cuts the corner at Foster Beck's entry into the Nidd, to a stile to the right of the prominent Brigg House Farm. Alongside a cottage a small footbridge crosses the beck, now followed upstream to a gate before striking across to the next gate onto a junction of lanes at Corn Close.

Turn left along the road down-dale to reach the Watermill Inn. Its magnificent waterwheel is over 10 metres in diameter, an iron and wood structure that was restored with pride in 1990 after years of neglect. Steps lead from the car park to a precariously perched millpond, with ducks and donkeys in evidence. The wheel once served this former flax mill that itself operated as a ropemakers into the 1960s: conversion to an inn saw a chequered existence. Having once been a locally renowned folk music venue, it now takes full advantage of its spacious grounds and unique setting to draw a clientele that includes, quite naturally, many families.

Return to the junction and take the side road to Heathfield. This soon begins a steady climb to arrive at the scattered group of dwellings. This ancient settlement once had a fulling mill under the auspices of the monks of Byland Abbey, while the once important Yorke family smelted ore here from their lead mines.

Approaching the first buildings, opt for the drive down to the right to Spring Hill Farm. The diverted path skirts the right-hand exterior of the buildings and yard and winds round to a stile at the far end of the field. Up-dale are fine views of the finger-like Gouthwaite Reservoir, a birdwatcher's paradise. Constructed in 1901, the 25 m high dam is well camouflaged by foliage, which sets the scene for the least intrusive of the Nidderdale reservoirs. A mostly naturally wooded shoreline masks the harshness of man's hand: indeed, it could be argued that this is merely a return to colder times, when a glacial lake filled the dale floor here.

Wath Bridge.

From the stile descend half-left through two large fields, then straight over two smaller ones to drop steeply to the road at Wath lane end. Turn along the side road for Wath, crossing the bridge over the Nidd immediately, a lovely arched structure embowered in greenery. Widened a century ago, Wath Bridge maintains sufficient character to recall the days when it served the monks of Fountains Abbey and the packhorse trade.

The Sportsman's Arms, incidentally, is just along the road in the tiny, unspoilt hamlet, in a leafy setting just past the old station house and boasting a fine individual sign. The old station confirms the presence of a disused railway line, now merely a grassy embankment which you will soon be joining. Across the bridge take a contrastingly simple footbridge on the right, from where a path crosses a field to a stile, continuing on to meet the unmistakable course of the old railway.

The River Nidd at Pateley Bridge.

The Nidd Valley Light Railway was opened in 1908 by Bradford Corporation to convey material and men for the construction of the Angram dam at the dalehead. It also operated for two decades as a passenger line, but completion of the Scar House dam in 1936 saw the end of its useful life.

From the next stile the line is followed for some distance, to a point where the Nidd comes within a stone's throw. Beyond a stile in this tree-shrouded setting the railway is forsaken for the river, whose wooded bank leads unerringly back to Pateley Bridge. Part-way along, note the lively confluence caused by arrival of Foster Beck, where a green island sits in the centre of things. On reaching a weir, the path becomes confined and is deflected away to emerge between buildings onto a short lane immediately adjacent to Pateley's graceful bridge.

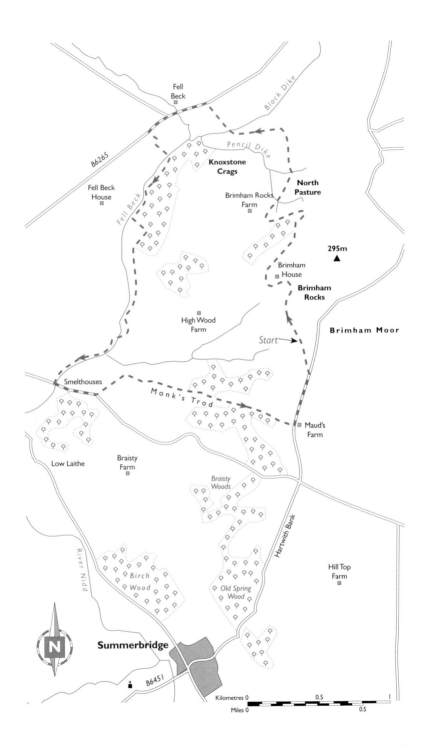

BRIMHAM ROCKS – THE GREATEST PLAYGROUND

I n the care of the National Trust, Brimham Rocks are the pride of Nidderdale. The valley's most famous visitor attraction has been drawing the crowds for more than two centuries, during which time little but the ownership has changed. Scores of weirdly sculpted sandstone rocks (better known locally as Millstone Grit) decorate colourful acres of moorland and woodland, the finest natural playground in the Dales. The rocks we see today were formed millions of years ago, yet only after the passing of the Ice Age were they left isolated and vulnerable. Then the harsher elements of Pennine weather set to work, as rain, wind and frost exposed the weaker lines in between. This process continues today, with each passing winter further eroding the sandstone fissures. Many of the rocks have acquired descriptive names, some easily recognisable, others rather fanciful. The surrounding countryside, however, is also of the highest standard, as this excursion will readily prove.

From the car park a broad carriageway leads directly to Brimham House. This gets the walk off to a proper start, saving the attractions of the intervening wonderland for journey's end. Formerly the Rocks House, it was built in 1792 by Lord Grantley for his moor keeper. It serves as a shop and information point, with refreshments and toilets alongside.

Resume by taking the main path left of the house. Further named outcrops are encountered, including the Dancing Bear (immediately) and Idol Rock. Easy location of these will instil confidence for the countless rocks awaiting identification on return to the main group at the end of the walk. Beyond the last rocks the path loops back to the right: leave it by a narrow green path which maintains the northerly aim and drops down to join a wider path. Turn left on it; keeping left at a fork it leads onto a farm drive on the moor edge.

INFORMATION

Distance: 8 km (5 miles).

Start and finish: Brimham Rocks. Large National Trust car park on the minor road linking B6165 and B6265 above Summerbridge (Grid ref. SE 208645).

Terrain: Mixed walking, good paths. Boots advisable.

Public transport: Seasonal weekend bus service from Harrogate. The Harrogate-Pateley Bridge bus can be used to begin the walk from Low Laithe, just off route near Smelthouses.

Refreshments: Cafe/ refreshments near the start; pub at Fell Beck.

Opening hours: *Brimham House:* Open Easter, Apr-May, Sat-Sun only, 1100–1700; Jun-Oct, daily 1100–1700.

Brimham Rocks.

Dancing Bear, Brimham Rocks.

Double back left on this rough road, passing through woods to approach Brimham Rocks Farm (High North Pasture Farm on maps). Before it, however, leave the drive at the first gate on the right after the trees. Cross to a gateway at the far end, then on again to a gate in the far right corner in front of North Pasture Farm. Enter the yard by another gate, and leave by one on the left after the main buildings.

Bear right across the field to a stile in a fence by a tiny stream. Continue on to a gate at the head of a green lane. Turn down it between enclosing walls and remain on its pleasant course (ignore a branch right) as it winds down to cross Fell Beck before rising onto a road. Descend left to the hamlet of Fell Beck, featuring the Half Moon Inn.

Continue up the road as it climbs away, just as far as the first farm road to the left. Pass between the buildings of Knoll Top to a gate, then swing right to a stile. Descend wall-side to another stile, then turn right above Fell Beck to a gateway. A clearer path through the trees remains well above the beck to the next fence. From the left-hand stile it drops to accompany the beck above a dam and a weir, as far as a walled track from the right. Here double back left down to a footbridge, remaining in the wood by turning right on a gradually rising path.

On approaching a walled enclosure the path forks: turn down to the right (without entering the field), the path soon continuing on the level to leave the trees at a stile below the isolated buildings of Low Wood. A thin path heads away to join a wider one descending from the left. Ignore a branch down to the beck, but remain on a level green way to enter birchwoods. The path eventually meets another, just past a stile. Follow it down to the right to a footbridge, and trace the beck downstream to emerge into Smelthouses.

Smelthouses is a charming hamlet in a setting to match. Graceful dwellings stand near the beck, where as early as the 14th century lead ore was smelted by the monks of Fountains Abbey. These were later joined by several flax mills, possibly the earliest in the district. It is difficult to imagine this sequestered spot as a hive of activity.

Turn left over the bridge and up the road as far as a drive on the left at Wysing House. Just past Low Wood House the track swings left. Leave it by a gate on the right to follow a wide, gradually rising green track. This is a former monks' trod on one of the cross-country trade routes radiating from Fountains Abbey. Mostly enclosed, it later follows a fence to arrive at a gate where High Wood comes up. Beyond a gate a path heads up through the pasture to a gateway in the wall on the right, then soon leaves the trees to rise to the left. Through another gateway and along a field-side, typical Brimham country is now dominant. One more gate is met before reaching the road.

Heading left onto Brimham Moor, the drive back to the car park leaves the road to finish the walk, though an earlier fork sees a branch remain on the moor to escape the road a little earlier. Time to go exploring! The mightiest of the rocks are serious cliff faces, and these occur at the western edge of the moor, overlooking the valley. Here rock climbers are very likely to be found in various improbable positions. Those that can perform in front of a crowd are likely to look the most comfortable.

Brimham Rocks.

Back in the heart of things, can you identify the Eagle Rock or the Turtle Rock, the Blacksmith and Anvil and the Druid's Writing Desk, or the Cannon Rocks and Castle Rocks? Perhaps you'll think up your own names for them!

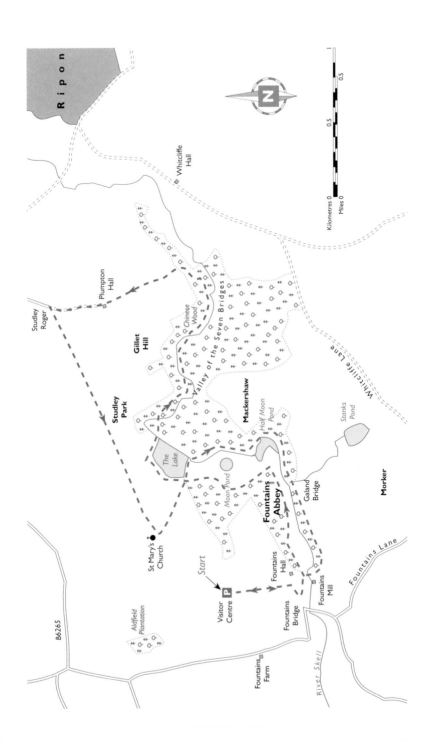

MEDIEVAL MAJESTY – FOUNTAINS ABBEY

Fountains Abbey and Studley Royal bear the prestigious designation of World Heritage Site: though the walk isn't demanding, the need to savour the wonders of this place certainly is. Don't pencil this in for a half-day!

Amongst various literature on sale at the visitor centre, two modestly priced leaflets depict the layout and history of the abbey itself, and the spacious grounds and their many features. From the visitor centre, descend the path to reach the side of Fountains Hall. The magnificent hall with its intricate facade was completed in 1611, much of the stone coming from the abbey that had only been abandoned in 1539. Last private owners were the Vyner family, with much evidence of their presence – note a touching memorial in the entrance stairway.

INFORMATION

Distance: 8 km (5 miles).

Start and finish: Fountains Abbey, 3 km west of Ripon. There is a large car park at the visitor centre, signposted off the B6265.

Terrain: Parkland walking, light footwear normally adequate, though a short woodland section can get muddy.

Refreshments: Cafes at the start and mid-walk.

Opening hours: *Fountains Abbey* is open as follows: Apr-Sep 1000–1900, Oct-Mar 1000–1700 (or dusk). Closed Christmas Eve, Christmas Day, and Fridays in January, November and December. Admission charge (National Trust members free). *St Mary's Church:* Easter week and Apr-Sep, daily 1300–1700.

Fountains Abbey.

Back on the main carriageway, turn left to explore the delights of this staggeringly beautiful ruin, the most extensive Cistercian remains in England. Fountains Abbey was founded in 1132 by Benedictine monks from St Mary's Abbey in York: seeking a stricter regime, they turned to the French Cistercian order. Built largely between the mid 12th and 13th centuries, this was one of the most important and wealthy religious houses. Whilst their farms (called granges) occupied much of nearby Nidderdale, their possessions stretched across to the Cumberland fells. Dairy farming and lead mining also came within their scope, and many peoples' lives revolved around the abbey. Perhaps its finest feature is the 100 m long west range, with its vaulted cellarium. Most impressive, however, is the 60 m high tower, a 16th century addition built by Abbot Marmaduke Huby: it was never completed.

Rejoining the main carriageway, a superb walk leads along to the water gardens, also regarded as the finest in the country. Since the Trust's acquisition of the estate in the 1980s, the gardens have seen extensive restoration, and once again resemble the beautiful scene created throughout the 1700s by the Aislabie family. Buildings such as the temples and the Octagon Tower were added during this period.

Beyond a bend above Half Moon Pond, running above the canalised River Skell, you are treated to views over the Moon Pond, flanked by crescents and with lead statues in attendance, to the Temple of Piety. High above, meanwhile, are other features for the return journey. At the eastern end of the grounds another shop and ticket office see you emerge at the lake and Studley Royal deer park. Here also are cafe and toilets.

Follow the drive alongside the lake, and at the end fork right on a track to the outflow. Here begins the walk through the Valley of the Seven Bridges, the first being a wooden one over the outflow. The Skell is accompanied downstream through the encroaching walls of this steep-sided valley, a delightful amble that recrosses the river on five further occasions on identical stone arched bridges. After the last one the estate is vacated at a deer-proof gate. A woodland path runs down to pass the seventh bridge (this plain structure is not crossed) before the track climbs the wooded bank. Out of the trees it runs a pleasant field-side course with open views.

Passing Plumpton Hall, the track becomes surfaced to reach the edge of Studley Roger at a lodge. Here go left on the estate drive, through the East Entrance arch to re-enter the park along a broad driveway. St Mary's church is framed beyond a long avenue of limes. In the heart of the centuries-old deer park you can see red, fallow and Sika deer.

When cars are sent left to the car park above the lake, either go with them, or incorporate a visit to the church by remaining on the drive. St Mary's was built in 1871–78, boasting an impressive spire prominent in many local views. From the church a path descends to the abbey's east entrance by the lake.

Temple of Piety, at Fountains Abbey.

Re-entering, turn immediately left and cross the Skell as it enters the lake. The path heads back alongside the water gardens, but just before the Temple of Piety, a higher level alternative offers itself. Slanting back up, pass through the Serpentine Tunnel to emerge by the Octagon Tower. This provides good views over the Moon Pond and much of the grounds. Continuing, the broad path runs on past the Temple of Fame to the Surprise View at Anne Boleyn's Seat.

The 'surprise' at this wooden shelter is the sudden return of the abbey to the scene, dramatically beyond a length of the river. Just past here the path doubles back down the wooded bank to rejoin the lower one at Half Moon Pond. Turning left, the way runs on by the river to return to the abbey, passing Robin Hood's Well en route. You can turn down to the start of the ruins for further exploration, or remain on the path above the abbey to arrive at a museum and refreshment kiosk. Here the path returns to join the outward carriageway.

INDEX

Opposite: River Skell at Fountains Abbey.

Other titles in this series

Other titles in preparation

Long distance guides published by HMSO

HMSO Bookshops
71 Lothian Road, Edinburgh EH3 9AZ
0131-228 4181 Fax 0131-229 2734
49 High Holborn, London WC1V 6HB
(counter service only)
0171-873 0011 Fax 0171-831 1326
68–69 Bull Street, Birmingham B4 6AD
0121-236 9696 Fax 0121-236 9699
33 Wine Street, Bristol BS1 2BQ
0117 9264306 Fax 0117 9294515
9-21 Princess Street, Manchester M60 8AS
0161-834 7201 Fax 0161-833 0634
16 Arthur Street, Belfast BT1 4GD
01232 238451 Fax 01232 235401
The HMSO Oriel Bookshop, The Friary, Cardiff CF1 4AA
01222 395548 Fax 01222 384347

HMSO publications are available from:

HMSO Publications Centre
(Mail, fax and telephone orders only)
PO Box 276, London SW8 5DT
Telephone orders 0171-873 9090
General enquiries 0171-873 0011
(queuing system in operation for both numbers)
Fax orders 0171-873 8200

HMSO's Accredited Agents
(see Yellow Pages)

and through good booksellers

Printed in Scotland for HMSO by c.c. No. 70343 50C 4/96